Endorsements

For single, seriously dating, or married couples, this book is a must-have, because it will challenge your perspective regarding marriage. With thought-provoking questions and personal stories, Richard takes a look at marriage from a business and leadership perspective.

The premise of the book is that in order to have a successful marriage, you have to become intentional, beginning with understanding your *why, what,* and *how.*

— Colie B. Young III, Public Affairs Officer
United States Marine Corps

Marriage & Relationship Success

IT'S INTENTIONAL

Richard E. Hellen

SPIRIT-LED PUBLISHING

Richard E. Hellen
richardhellenpathways@gmail.com
www.rhpathways.com

Ordering Information:
Quantity sales. Special discounts are available on quantity purchases by corporations, associations, and others. For details, contact Richard E. Hellen at the address above.

Cover photo by Caroline Veronez
Cover design by Pixel Studio
Copy editing by Sally Hanan of Inksnatcher.com
Bio and couple head shot by suzannecovert.com
Book layout ©2013 BookDesignTemplates.com

Marriage & Relationship Success: It's Intentional/Richard E. Hellen.
—1st ed.
ISBN 978-1-943011-98-8

For my wife, Kim; my children, Kanesha, Lashunda, and Jahari;

and my mentors,

Poppy and Mommy Santos, and Harry and Lendy Jones.

Contents

THE SECRET: The only way marriage succeeds is when two people work together for the same common goal and are willing to make the necessary sacrifices for the goal's obtainment. To achieve the target, we must choose to be teammates vs. roommates. Teammates work together and share the same common goal, whereas roommates share the same common space. Becoming teammates is the key ingredient in the recipe for a successful marriage.

Introduction

Marriage is simple; the complexity lies in keeping it that way.

This book is dedicated to showing how longevity with contentment is possible when success in marriage becomes intentional. You can have the marriage you have always envisioned; however, what you want and what you are willing to give up have to be in agreement.

In the book of Genesis, Moses wrote, "And the Lord God said it is not good that the man should be alone; I will make him an help meet for him" (Genesis 2:18). From the very beginning God created us with a desire to share our existence with someone else; however, that particular verse doesn't indicate how we can coexist in harmony. In the upcoming chapters, my desire is to demonstrate how coexisting in harmony is not only possible but can become our reality. Yes, success is possible when we become intentional, deliberate, intending, and purposeful. Being intentional increases our chances of succeeding and decreases our chances of becoming another divorce statistic.

I'm confident that by the time you reach the end of this book, you will have a clearer picture of what a healthy marriage is composed of, and you will be able to slowly implement some of our processes and procedures in your relationship. Whether you use our processes, tweak our processes, or create your own, my desire is for you to experience your relationship on another level.

We invest in the stock market, cars, and houses, but our relationships will not bear fruit unless we make intentional investments in them. The mere fact that you are reading this book indicates you are serious about investing in your marriage, so you can expect a significant return. As Zig Ziglar says, *See you at the top.*

Love you all,

Richard and Kim Hellen

TEAM HELLEN

CHAPTER 1

Marriage Is a Business

Mergers are like marriages. They are the bringing together of two individuals. If you wouldn't marry someone for the "operational efficiencies" they offer in the running of a household, then why would you combine two companies with unique cultures and identities for that reason? ~ Simon Sinek

When companies assume that joining forces with another company will be beneficial for all parties, they form what is called a merger, in which two companies come together to form one company under the same name. Although this appears advantageous from the outside, between 70 to 90 percent of all mergers don't succeed, according to Clayton M. Christensen and Harvard Business Review (2016).

If certain things are not established before the merger transpires, it will not prosper, no matter how advantageous things appear from the outside. Before merging a business, leaders must proceed with caution and move forward only when both parties have a united purpose that supersedes personal gain. So what's the reasoning behind the failure of most mergers?

> Lack of a shared vision
> Flawed intentions
> Poor communication
> Inability to combine two separate and distinct cultures.

LACK OF A SHARED VISION

If couples have separate visions for the marriage and are not traveling down the same road, it is impossible to end up at the same destination. Our path determines our destination and not our intentions. We can have the best of intentions, but if we are heading in the wrong direction, we will end up in the wrong place.

This is the difference between being roommates and teammates. Roommates share the same space, but teammates share the same common goals. Where are we going?

FLAWED INTENTIONS

> If I marry her, she can pay some of my bills, which will alleviate my financial burdens.
> If I'm married, I no longer have to look for a sexual partner, nor feel condemned for having sex out of wedlock.

> If I marry him, my son will have a male figure in the household to respect.

The key component in each statement is *I* and *my*, and not *us* and *we*. We must enter the merger for the right reasons and with the right intentions to obtain the right outcome.

LACK OF COMMUNICATION

It's not uncommon for couples to enter marriage and assume certain things without ever conversing with their spouses, such as how they will save money or their approach to sex, religion, or parenting. When these issues surface, they create hardship for the marriage, because one party assumed that the spouse viewed these issues in the same light. We must communicate on every pressing issue and leave nothing to assumption.

COMBINING TWO CULTURES

When it comes to leadership, culture is one of my favorite topics, because I think it is one of the most vital elements within an organization, one that will determine its level of success.

The word "culture" is usually used in relation to organizations or people groups; however, each person has his own individual culture—his attitudes, beliefs, and behaviors. The merger of two people with different beliefs and behaviors, who are unaware that relationships are about giving, understanding, compromise, and working toward a common goal, will be disastrous for the relationship. The culture that exists within the relationship will determine if a couple succeeds, fails, or coexists.

It's imperative that we know who we are, who we are attempting to merge with, and that our end goals are the same. If not, we will become part of the 90 percent of mergers that do not succeed.

> *What can make the difference toward succeeding and minimizing our chances of failure? What we know, and what we do with what we know.*

Potential Candidates

When companies post an ad for an employment opportunity, they seem to be very clear regarding what they are looking for in a potential candidate. They give a detailed listing of what I call their must-haves and preferred qualifications for the position. These requirements include things such as:

a bachelor's degree,
five years of experience, and
the ability to travel.

The organization might *prefer* the candidate to have a master's degree, but it would not disqualify him or her from consideration. Companies are sticklers about their must-haves, and usually will not consider someone for the position without those minimum requirements. These must-haves set the standard from the very beginning for what the company is willing and not willing to accept. Without these standards, companies will not have a clear picture of their preferred candidate, which could make the hiring process elusive.

> *If we don't know what we are looking for, we will not recognize it when it appears.*

Changing How We Approach Marriage

What if we approached dating and marriage with a business mindset? It could eliminate years of heartache, disappointment, and divorce. When people are preparing to start a company, they create a business plan, mission statement, vision statement, and list of core values. These define who they are, where they want to go, and what they hope to accomplish upon arrival. This is how companies establish purpose and direction.

What would happen if every marriage had a success plan (business plan), mission statement, vision statement, and list of core values?

> Could this give our marriages purpose, direction, and intentionality?
> Could this make for healthier marriages?
> Would this allow us to see marriage more as a partnership than a relationship?

There are countless books by people who have more degrees and status than I could ever imagine. I believe what's missing in most books and relationship training is the absence of leadership regarding marriage. Yes, leadership. Anytime leadership is excluded from anything, failure will be the by-product. John Maxwell (2007) states "everything rises and falls on leadership." One of the major tenets of leadership is to provide purpose and direction. [NOTE FOR MEN: I will discuss this in greater detail in chapter 5, but one of a woman's basic needs is leadership. If we are not providing purpose and direction, it will be challenging to get our spouses or our children to follow. No one has a desire to follow someone who is oblivious to where he is going and how he will get there.]

I am going to expose principles that will begin that process. Not only will you have greater success in your marriage, but your greatest joy will stem from your sharing what you have learned with other couples. Success transpires when you have a purpose, systems, and processes that can be duplicated. These leadership principles can be used at work, church, school, or your nonprofit organization, because leadership principles are transferable to any environment.

Why duplication? One of life's secrets to success is our ability to help and serve others. I frequently ask people who have been married for many years what the key to their success is, and I rarely receive a specific answer. Since I teach on leadership, I believe firmly in duplicative processes and systems. Anytime we are unsure of how we arrived at our success, that success will remain unduplicatable. It's hard to put the relationship back on track if we are nebulous about what was keeping it afloat. If you ask the average man what the purpose of his marriage is, you will probably get a blank stare. Having a purpose is foreign to most people; however, I think it's the oxygen that all marriages are missing. As you dive further into this book, I hope to explain the necessity of looking at marriage through this lens. Just think, by the time you finish this book, your marriage will be operating with a clear purpose and a defined destination.

Company's Qualification List

Most companies know what they desire in a potential candidate and will not settle for something less. Job ads on

LinkedIn, Monster, etc. give long lists of required and preferred qualifications. These qualities, skills, and education are nonnegotiable. Unlike companies, we often don't have a clear picture of our must-haves and our preferred qualities for our potential partners. Today we live in a superficial society, and our must-haves often start and stop with aesthetics. We have sometimes become so enamored with the outside of the car that we miss that the engine is the most critical component.

I find it surprising that companies hire based on education, skills, and experience but terminate based upon character—the attributes or features that make up and distinguish an individual. Just maybe corporations and people in America have the most important thing last. Since companies fire and relationships end because of character, it seems like we should begin with good character as our number one must-have.

We can train for a skill, but we cannot train for character. Change in any area of life is challenging and is usually invoked by some life-altering event. Most people will not change until they hurt enough or have had enough. We can desperately desire change for those we love, but change will not transpire until they desperately desire to change for themselves.

What Are We Looking For?

A friend of mine asked me to assist her in finding someone to date. I asked her what she was looking for. She stated, "Someone who is six foot tall, six-pack, and easy on the eyes." Nothing is wrong with that, except those qualities should never supersede character. This reminded me of when King

Solomon was appointed king of Israel at a very young age. Knowing the responsibility that comes with being a king, Solomon asked God for "an understanding heart to judge thy people, that I may discern between good and bad: for who is able to judge this thy so great a people?" (1 Kings 3:9). His speech pleased God, because he did not ask for long life or riches; therefore, God blessed him with fame, riches, and honor.

I believe that when we make character a priority, God might just bless us with some of those other physical attributes. However, if not, nothing on the outside should ever supersede what's on the inside, because what we see in a man's appearance is not nearly as important as what we see in his heart. If we fail to make character a priority in the beginning, we will face his character in the end.

Character matters.

"For out of the heart proceed evil thoughts, murders, adulteries, fornications, thefts, false witness, blasphemies" (Matthew 15:19). Having a trophy husband or wife who exhibits these traits makes for a miserable and pretentious marriage. Couples have to pretend to be content in public while they suffer in private. When these couples announce they are getting a divorce, it takes everyone by surprise, because they have faked contentment during their entire marriage. Choose this day who you will serve—character or aesthetics. As for me and my house, I'm starting with what's on the inside.

What are your nonnegotiables or must-haves?

What are some things you desire but are not must-haves?

Is the outside more important than the inside? Does character supersede looks?

If you had to choose between character and aesthetics, which one wins and why?

Anytime we are not clear on our must-haves, we enter into what I refer to as *the settling zone.* We settle for being in a relationship crippled by our insecurities and lack of clarity. It is imperative that we can define our must-haves and be unwilling for them to be compromised. Once we consent to compromise, we have accepted the relationship on the other person's term. Cheating, lying, disrespect, etc. will be acceptable because we will make a bed for his or her behavior. What we tolerate is what we teach.

We can't control what someone else does; we can only control how we respond. A young lady once told me her boyfriend was verbally abusing her. How did we get to abuses—plural? The first time should have been the last time, but if not, we have just informed him or her that this type of behavior is acceptable. If we are not aware of our worth, we will settle for less. Know what you are looking for by knowing what you are willing and not willing to accept. Remember, no one can mistreat you without your consent. What are your *must-haves?*

Do you make excuses for people's behavior?

Do you believe their behavior is your fault?

The question is never why he or she does this to you; it's why are you willing to accept it?

My Background

From as early as I can remember, I grew up with very little self-worth and low self-esteem. I played sports and made associations, seeking acceptance from my parents as well as my peers. I will never forget the day we were playing basketball on the playground, and I was laughing at a joke someone had told. Robert Lee, one of the neighborhood kids, stated, "Man, you are ugly as hell with your laugh." For years after that, I covered my mouth every time I laughed. I allowed someone else's perception of me to define and control me.

I yearned for the day to hear my parents say I'm proud of you and we love you. Much to my dismay, my parents went to their grave without expressing those words to me. Unfortunately, my parents were never validated by their parents, so they did not know how to validate me. In most cases, we will be and do what we have seen and experienced. They provided food, water, shelter, and clothing, and that was their way of showing love. This lack of validation caused me to spend my entire youth and part of my adulthood seeking acceptance. As a result, anytime a woman said she loved me, I assumed that meant we should get married. I mentioned earlier that one of the reasons mergers fail is flawed intentions. I was using them to validate me.

By the time I met Kim, I had been through three practice marriages and several failed relationships. I call them practice marriages because I had no idea what I was doing and didn't take my vows seriously. I dated and married people for all the wrong reasons, and when the relationships failed, I blamed the other person. It was much easier for me to blame the other person than to accept responsibility. It wasn't until years later that I understood that placing blame does not hurt them, but it hurt me. I couldn't grow and change by looking at them; I could only grow and change when I started to look within.

I thought it was my wife's job to make me complete, and her responsibility to fix my brokenness!

However, one day I woke up and realized that *I* was responsible for not succeeding relationally, and I had to fix my brokenness. Victims of sexual abuse often grow up and become sexually abusive to others. However, once exposed, they cannot use the excuse that they abused others because they were abused. They have to pay the cost for their actions. So did I. I had to learn to take lemons and make lemonade.

The day I accepted responsibility was the day I began to mature and grow as a man. As I started to work on me, who I was and what I wanted became apparent for the first time in my life. I was confident about what I wanted, as well as what I was not willing to accept. Failing is not failing if at some point we fail forward.

What have you learned from your past experiences?

Success in marriage doesn't just happen; it has to be intentional. Being intentional is a mindset that can change the trajectory of any relationship. Our beliefs drive our behavior. When we change what we believe, we change what we do, because our beliefs drive our behavior.

My Growth

Because I suffer from low self-esteem, I had become accustomed to settling for any relationship. Little did I know that these experiences would later cause me to recognize what I was willing and not willing to accept. People often say experience is the best teacher, but I say evaluated experience is. My lessons had become my teacher, and I had become a good student. For the first time in my life, I was ready to teach people how I wanted to be treated by how I treated them. I finally knew who I was and, more importantly, whose I was. I'm the son of the King.

Marriage is like a business, and just as successful businesses are clear on what they are willing and not willing to accept in a potential candidate, we need to set the standards at the beginning. When we do, we will not have to try and fix them in the end.

Know what you want.

With this decision to clarify what I was looking for in advance, and to cement those boundaries in place before taking on anything new, I decided that whoever I chose to marry would be the one for life, and the only way I could make it work would be to have those boundaries and decisions set in place before we ever went to the altar. And this is what Kim and I put together as a result.

A Mission Statement

A mission statement is a written declaration of an organization's core purpose and focus that typically remains unchanged over time.

PROPERLY CRAFTED MISSION STATEMENTS:

1) Serve as filters to separate what is important from what is not
2) Communicate a sense of intended direction to the entire organization
3) Consist of three components:
   a. It's simple
   b. It's portable
   c. It's repeatable

When the marriage faces an impasse, the mission statement serves as the foundation, which guides a couple to higher ground through a higher purpose. The conversation shifts from what the couple is experiencing to what is it that they are trying to accomplish. Temporary experiences and feelings are about the person having them, whereas the goal a couple is trying to achieve is far greater.

Getting married takes little to no effort; however, staying married is where the challenge exists. When I ask couples for their vision, mission, or plan for success, almost invariably I get a deer in the headlights look. Most couples do not have a written mission and vision statement for their marriage. Neither the vast majority of marriage seminars, or premarital counseling, emphasize the importance of couples having a clear purpose for their marriage, so why is it so important? King Solomon, the wisest man of his time, said, "Where there is no vision, the people perish" (Proverbs 29:18).

If there is no mission and vision for the marriage, the relationship will merely exist rather than flourish with purpose and direction.

TEAM HELLEN MISSION STATEMENT

To have a lasting marriage worthy of emulation, and to always look to our heavenly Father, as we are fully conscious of where our guidance will come from.

TEAM HELLEN

A Vision Statement

TEAM HELLEN VISION STATEMENT

To stay committed by serving one another and not serving ourselves, while placing the needs of each other above our own needs. We pray that as God looks down upon this commitment, he says well done, thou good and faithful servants.

TEAM HELLEN

A vision statement is a description of what an organization would like to achieve in the mid-term or long-term future.

OUR CORE VALUES FOR MARRIAGE

- Honesty
- Commitment
- Selflessness

- Growth

A marriage that starts off with a clear mission, vision, list of core values, and an understanding that marriage is work has a greater chance of experiencing long-term success. If we approach marriage with a different perspective, I'm confident we will produce a different result. Marriage is a business.

What is your mission statement?

What is your vision statement?

What are your core values?

The Challenge for Some Businesses

Some companies ask for more than they are willing to offer; therefore, you should be skeptical about asking someone to have traits and qualities you don't possess. Why is this important? You don't attract who you *want;* you attract who you *are.* If you desire someone who is honest, trustworthy, dependable, and hard-working, do you have those same qualities? Because as you seek those qualities in others, they will be seeking the same qualities in you. Are you the person you want the other person to be? Do you have the character traits you are looking for in some else?

Takeaways

- Most mergers fail because of lack of vision, communication, flawed intentions, and trying to combine two separate and distinct cultures. Most relationships fail because of lack of vision, communication, flawed intentions, and trying to combine two separate and distinct cultures.
- Character is made up of the attributes and qualities distinctive to an individual.
- You can train for skill, but you can't train for character.
- Character is more important than aesthetics.
- Companies hire based upon skill, education, and experience but fire based upon character.
- Relationships end because of some character flaw.
- Know what you are willing and unwilling to accept.
- Never make excuses for your behavior or someone else's.

CHAPTER 2

Spiritual Agreement

Without purpose there can be no direction, and without direction, there cannot be a common destination.

There are five prerequisites to creating direction and purpose for your marriage (leadership) as well as to establishing your nonnegotiables and must-haves.

"Can two walk together, except they be agreed?" (Amos 3:3).

You don't have to be a religious person to understand this principle.

For me and my house, spiritual agreement is #1.

It is impossible to have success in any endeavor in which people are not in agreement. However, this particular text does not indicate any agreed-upon topics. I have taken the liberty to create five prerequisites that, if agreed to before and during the marriage, will lead to years of fulfillment. By no means does this list indicate a marriage free from conflict, but it will set the foundation for healthy responses to circumstances, so that when the relationship faces adversity, it can still flourish.

As you look at this list, I want you to consider some of the reasons people separate or divorce. Think hard. Are you still thinking? Have you come to the conclusion that most divorces or separations will be because couples are not in agreement in one or more of these areas?

Spiritual agreement
Financial agreement
Parental agreement
Sexual agreement
Emotional agreement

My petition is for every couple to be madly in love and happier today than yesterday.

When someone asks you if you are married, I want you to be able to respond with an emphatic *no* and then say you are *happily* married and not just married. This is possible when both people are going in the same direction, desiring the same outcome, operating with the same purpose, and embracing the five agreements above.

Spiritual Agreement

> *Know God, know peace; no God, no peace.*

I am a firm believer that God has to be the nucleus and foundation of every relationship. When someone builds a house, the foundation is the first and most important part of the home. If the foundation is not correct, nothing else will fit properly, and each additional part will have to be forced and modified. Having God as the nucleus of the relationship gives couples a sure foundation and the opportunity to serve something greater than themselves. If couples can't find something to serve that exceeds them, they worship and serve themselves. This leads to a relationship driven by selfishness. "Every way of a man is right in his own eyes: but the Lord pondereth the hearts" (Proverbs 21:2).

If I am my religion, that means that whatever I believe is correct based upon my standard of right and wrong. However, if I believe God is the authority for what's correct, it subjects me to something superior to self. When this transpires, God and his written Word become my true north.

If we are going to love our spouses, what will be our example of the way we should love? The Bible talks about how God is love and that his love came with the ultimate sacrifice of his son. "For God so loved the world, that He gave His only begotten Son, that whosoever believeth in Him should not perish, but have everlasting life" (John 3:16). Why is knowing this of any value to you? His love was designed to be our example of love—it came without conditions but was filled with sacrifice. If God is absent in the relationship, the love in the relationship will be based upon conditions and will come without sacrifice.

When I speak about God being the center, it comes with a two-fold responsibility. Most couples will say he is the center, but God doesn't surface in their marriage unless there is a crisis. God being our nucleus can't just be evident with words, it must also be evident in deed—we can say he is the core, but it must be demonstrated by our actions. "Dear children, let us not love with words or speech but with actions and in truth" (1John 3:18 NIV).

Will we be the center of our marriage or will God?

If God is not the center, what will be the guiding authority in the relationship?

What will be our example of love, and how should it be displayed?

One of Many Challenges

Let's say someone is a Jehovah's Witness and the other person is Baptist. These religions serve and honor God in many separate ways. Jehovah's Witnesses typically don't observe holidays, whereas in Christianity, holidays are an integral part of Christian tradition. Around Christmas and Easter, these distinct beliefs could create a severe amount of discomfort and tension in the home, especially with the children. Will we get the children gifts or will we forgo these gifts because of our religious beliefs?

How could this affect the children?

What stress could this potentially cause the marriage?

Will this create contentment or contention?

Questions such as:

Where will we get married?
Who will marry us?
What church will we attend?
Do I have to convert to your religion?

are all concerns that need to be addressed. Never go into the marriage assuming that someone is going to comply with your desires without mutual consent.

The Scripture emphasizes being equally yoked for good reason. There can be no success in marriage when God is in the background and not the forefront. Therefore, for me and my house, I couldn't consider dating or marrying someone who didn't express a passion, love, and desire for God to be our north star. Nor could I marry someone whose religious beliefs differed drastically from mine, because it would be a disaster waiting to unfold.

I have met people who married their spouses with the hope that they might one day give their lives to God and change their religious views. Hope for change is dangerous territory and often leads to disappointment. The day couples say *I do,* they agree to love each other for life—because of who they are on that day and not for what they hope the other can become. If you are not equally yoked, proceed with extreme caution and be willing to accept the consequences of your choice.

Living What We Say We Believe—the Ultimate Influencer

Our focus can't be on trying to change our spouses' religious beliefs, but about putting all of our efforts into improving ourselves. I believe one of the reasons it's difficult to get our spouses to church, or others, is *us.* If they see that church hasn't made a significant change in our lives, they will not be compelled to follow our lead. Paul stated, "If thou, being a Jew, livest after the manner of the Gentiles, and not as do the Jews, why compellest thou the Gentiles to live as the Jews do?" (Galatians 2:14). However, when people see we have changed, it has the power to change them, and it's called *influence.*

If we live a life that reflects our beliefs, our spouses or significant others should be asking us about our religion and the source of our disposition. If the life we live doesn't influence them to come, nothing we say will. We can nag our spouses and get them to come against their wills, but just remember, they will be of the same opinion still. Our goal should always be to influence and inspire but never to force.

> *Do you and your spouse, or significant other, have the same religious beliefs? If not, how do your religions differ?*
>
> *If they differ, what problems do you experience or perceive?*

Doctrines

What would the church be like if we embraced love more than religion? From the moment your religion differs from someone else's, you feel distance and division. If a couple says they are Catholic, we tend to look at the things they believe versus what we believe and compare. What if our common bond was love and not what we believed? I don't mean we have to change our beliefs, but we can choose to not allow what we believe to separate us into silos.

> *Don't tell me about your religion, show me your love. Religion divides and separates whereas love unites and is the only universal language. If I never see your love, I will never embrace your faith.*

> Though I speak with the tongues of men and of angels, and have not charity, I am become *a*ssounding brass, or a tinkling cymbal. And though I have *the gift*

> *of* prophecy, and understand all mysteries, and all knowledge; and though I have all faith, so that I could remove mountains, and have not charity, I am nothing. And though I bestow all my goods to feed *the poor,* and though I give my body to be burned, and have not charity, it profiteth me nothing.
>
> — I Corinthians 13:1–3, emphasis mine

If we wore our love on our sleeves and not our religion, we would attract more people to Christ. People would see us as the church and not the building. The church can't be transformed until we are.

Does your spouse or do others see your religion first, or your love?

Do your beliefs draw your spouse closer or do they repel him or her?

At almost every baseball game, some attendee holds up a sign with the Scripture "For God so loved the world, that he gave his only begotten Son, that whosoever believeth in him should not perish, but have everlasting life" (John 3:16). The emphasis is that *God gave.* Love gives whereas lust takes.

Love is a verb and verbs represent *action.* If we say we love someone, our actions must be in direct agreement with our words. "One witness shall not rise up against a man for any iniquity, or for any sin, in any sin that he sinneth: at the mouth of two witnesses, or at the mouth of three witnesses, shall the matter be established" (Deuteronomy 19:15). Our first witness is when we confess our love, but the second witness is our demonstration of it. Both witnesses are necessary, and one without the other offers no validation or confirmation.

In the end, couples should agree that God is going to be the head of the relationship and will be the driving force for their success.

Takeaways

- Agree that God is the foundation of your marriage.
- Agree on how your religion will set the order of your celebrations.
- Make God's love in and through you both more important than religious rules.

CHAPTER 3

Divorce Is Not an Option

In every marriage more than a week old, there are grounds for divorce. The trick is to find, and continue to find, grounds for marriage. ~ Robert Anderson

I can remember going to the store with my mother as a child, and we would often run into some of her friends. After a few pleasantries, they would frequently ask my mom how my father was doing. She would state he was doing well, just working hard every day. I find it amazing that years later, among most circles of friends, that dialogue has completely changed. Today, if we see a woman we have not seen in a while, we sometimes ask if she is still married, and not how her husband is doing. Longevity in marriage is no longer expected, and giving up has become commonplace. However, with the right tools and guidance, it is possible to have the type of marriage your children or others will be proud to emulate.

A couple once came to me for counseling. My wife said she was sick of her husband and their relationship because all they would do was argue and fight, and that she didn't get married to come home every day to chaos. She wanted a divorce, because she felt she could do better by herself.

A Harsh Reality

About 50 percent of all marriages end in divorce, and according to Focus on the Family, blended families have a 60 percent divorce rate. Second marriages have about a 67 percent chance of divorce, and if you are on your third marriage, you have about a 75 percent chance of divorce.[1] When you look at these numbers, why would anyone even consider marriage? Regardless of the numbers, you can still succeed if you have the right tools and the right attitude.

Marriage is one of life's greatest treasures, yet finding success in marriage appears to be a great mystery. Fifty percent of marriages end in divorce, 30 percent of couples just coexist, and only about 20 percent of people are happily married. I know that might be hard to digest, but just take a closer look at the marriages in your inner circle. If you are like me, you see plenty of couples who are married, but very few who are madly in love.

Many people are beginning to wonder whether a successful marriage is possible, and in many cases, they have chosen to just cohabitate. Our trepidation toward marriage correlates to our perspectives—offered through social media, television, and our environment—which sometimes condones giving up and reinforces the lie that marriage doesn't work.

Once we learn to give up without giving a valid effort, quitting becomes easy. If we want marital success, it's simply a matter of becoming intentional about having a marriage that's driven by purpose.

What causes divorce in the first place? For each couple that divorces, this answer seems different. Some couples say it's finances or poor communication, while others refer to infidelity. However, none of these are the primary reason for divorce. These are all byproducts or symptoms and not the source of the problem. Couples spend years treating the symptoms and never get to the cause of the issue. So what is the number one cause of divorce if it is not finances, communication, or infidelity? One of the hardest truths to face in a relationship is coming to the reality that sometimes the iss-ue is-*u*.

Infidelity

When someone cheats, that's selfish. If someone hides money or spends money without considering the other party, that's selfish. Sexual gratification outside a marriage is selfish. If partners refuse to listen because they believe what they have to say is more important than what their other halves have to say, that's selfish.

Selfishness is about being only devoted to oneself—your interests, your needs being met, your welfare, etc., regardless of others' needs or desires. Selfishness is the *number one* cause of divorce, and every other issue couples face is a byproduct of selfishness. If you never fix the selfishness, other problems will show up somewhere else in the marriage. Eliminate the selfishness and you restore and strengthen the marriage.

Our Vows

I, Richard Hellen, take you, Kim Hellen, for my lawful wife—to have and to hold from this day forward, for better, for worse, for richer, for poorer, in sickness and health, until death do us part." ... I promise to be true to you in good times and in bad, in sickness and in health.

These are the vows husband and wife take during the ceremony, which is a covenant before God and man. The preacher or judge looks at the couple, and both emphatically agree to the terms without hesitation. The couple smiles and family members sit in admiration as their loved ones prepare for this lifelong commitment. The bride cries as she stares with respect at the love of her life. However, within a few weeks, months, and sometimes years, that look of admiration turns to resentment.

"For better" seems to have become "for worse."

What happened? It's called life, which is filled with ongoing challenges, and marriages not built on a solid foundation will succumb to those challenges. Somehow that feeling of marital bliss experienced on the wedding day has dissipated, and her cousin, Disappointment, has shown up at the home. Couples can quickly go from being excited about going home to looking for another home to go home to.

Trial and Error

After high school, I attended a local community college to major in mass communication. My high school teacher thought I was a good communicator and told me I should get into television or radio. I had no idea what I wanted to do after high school, so her recommendation sounded appealing. It's amazing how those who influence our lives can direct our paths. After two years of college and about twelve credit hours, I quietly realized that college was not in the cards. I eventually quit school to get a job at a local television station. Although I loved the job, it didn't pay enough money for me to move out of my mother's home. One day I was pondering my life, and I asked myself where I would be in five years. My answer concerned me.

> *If you don't know where you are going to be in the next five years, you are already there.*

The very next day I enlisted in the military, and thirty days later, I headed to basic training at Fort Leonard Wood, Missouri. After I had completed basic and advanced individual training, the Army sent me to Korea on a one-year duty assignment. One afternoon, while sitting in my barracks, I decided to write to my first girlfriend. Let's call her Lisa. We had dated for about two years during college but had broken up on rather bad terms. After she received my letter, we began to correspond frequently. It did not take long before we started considering getting back together. It's easy to forget that when we read the same book, the ending is the same. Nothing was going to be different because I was not different. It was evident that the military had changed me on the outside, but I was the same on the inside. I was still insecure, and I wanted to get together for all the wrong reasons (flawed intentions).

My time in Korea went fast, and soon I was back en route to Meridian, Mississippi, my hometown. I was excited to reunite with Lisa, as well as visit with some of my high school friends. I must admit, I was proud to be a soldier, and for the first time I felt my life had meaning.

After a brief stint of visiting my parents, I headed to see Lisa. We hit it off as if we had not missed a beat. However, after a few days I quickly released why we had broken up in the first place. We began to have frivolous disagreements that would last for hours, and by the time the arguments ended, we had forgotten the initial cause. As I mentioned earlier, when we are not confident in who we are, we make excuses for our behavior, as well as the other person's.

I was scheduled to be home for thirty days before heading to Fort Polk, Louisiana. After my second week of seeing Lisa, I asked her to marry me, despite all the evidence that nothing had changed within either of us. Excited as a new kid on the first day of school, I couldn't wait to tell my mom. Barely before I could get the words "We are getting married" out of my mouth, my mother began to cry. These were not tears of joy but of apprehension and trepidation. My mother had witnessed our frequent and explosive disagreements, so she was concerned about our decision to marry so abruptly. In retrospect, she had every right to be apprehensive and doubtful about our decision. I looked at my mother and said, "Mom, if it doesn't work out, I can always get a *divorce.*"

Lukewarm

"I know thy works, that thou art neither cold nor hot: I would thou wert cold or hot. So then because thou art lukewarm, and neither cold nor hot, I will spue thee out my mouth" (Revelation 3:15–16). *Hot* represents someone who is ready to marry with no reservations, whereas cold represents someone who is not ready or has reservations. I was lukewarm. Before the marriage commenced, I had one foot in the house and one foot on the steps.

Going into the marriage with divorce as an option will place more weight on the outside of the home than on the inside. The minute the relationship hits an impasse, we seek reasons to dissolve it and not ways to resolve it. If the marriage is to succeed, divorce can't be an option.

Why Have Adversity?

Despite what you might think, you are not the only couple to experience trials and tribulation. It is easy to throw a pity party when you believe your marriage should exclude adversity. Have you ever noticed that when you come across couples who have been married for a long time, they all have the same testimony? It usually begins with, "We've been married for xyz years, and it came with lots of trials and tribulations, but we persevered." In the famous words of Job: "But he said unto her, Thou speakest as one of the foolish women speaketh. What? shall we receive good at the hand of God, and shall we not receive evil? In all this did not Job sin with his lips" (Job 2:10). Trials are not created to destroy your marriage but to strengthen it—so the marriage can serve as an example, to you and other couples, that success is possible.

God has to use someone's marriage as an example. Why not yours? A marriage that has not experienced a test has no idea of its strength.

Love was never intended to exist without challenging conditions, but it *was* meant to exist with sacrifice. Where there is no sacrifice, there is no love, and where there is no love, there is no sacrifice. If love comes with conditions, it is not real love. When the Messiah died on the cross, his death did not come with conditions but rather sacrifice, grace, and mercy. Likewise, your success in marriage will depend on becoming acquainted with sacrifice, grace, and mercy. The Messiah dispensed grace and mercy to you, and you are to be a reflection of him. Grace and mercy have to be dispensed in your marriage.

> Is this marriage thing real?
> Do couples understand their vows?
> Are couples ready for such a commitment, or will this be another marriage of temporary convenience?
> Are couples hearing but not listening to their vows?

Hearing Versus Listening

There is a significant difference between hearing and listening. We all hear, but few people listen. If you finished high school, you might have taken a communication or speaking class. This class is designed to teach students speaking skills and prepare them to communicate in front of an audience. However, most people have never taken a listening class, which requires a different skill set. Hearing involves delivering sounds to the ears, whereas listening requires being intentional about understanding. It is easy to say that most people hear their vows, but when we look at our divorce rate, it's obvious very few listen to their vows.

Our vows explicitly say

for better,
for worse,
for richer,
for poorer,
in sickness and in health,
until death do us part.

Despite the storms the marriage will face, your commitment to each other should not end unless one or both parties have expired. However, the minute many relationships face adversity, couples separate or file for divorce.

What happened to the vows you took on the day you stood before God and man? What happened to this lifelong commitment that only lasted a few months or years? Can you honestly say you loved this person if giving up came or comes so easily?

How committed am I to my vows?

Is divorce an option for my marriage?

My Desire

If I had my way, every couple would have to go through premarital counseling, because this increases the chance of their marital success. Counseling can open up concerns and fears that couples are reluctant to bring to the table. During the early dating stages, love can cause couples to overlook the other person's issues, as well as their behavior. Counseling often exposes these issues and deals with them before, rather than after, the marriage.

If this was Richard's world, every couple would have to attend counseling every six months for a minimum of four weeks. I refer to this as a marriage tune-up. This would create support and accountability on a continual basis for the marriage. Unfortunately, when most people think to seek advice, it's usually when the marriage has hit a major impasse. So much damage has been done that it is challenging to repair. However, when counseling becomes standard protocol, we get to resolve many issues before they become a crisis.

Challenge with Tune-Up Counseling

My wife and I went for counseling a few years ago, and the counselor asked what he could help us with. When I said we were there for a tune-up and nothing was wrong, he appeared confused. He was so accustomed to couples coming to him in a crisis mode that he was perplexed on how to proceed. We ended up (spending the time we were paying for) counseling him on how to handle some of his issues.

Just ensure that you find a good counselor—one who knows how to get both couples talking by asking the right questions and doesn't talk about his or her problems. Choose your counselor wisely.

For couples who might be reluctant to go to counseling, those couples could participate in a mentorship program. Most faith-based organizations have premarital counseling, but after the marriage, couples are left to fend for themselves. Every church should have a mentorship program that connects newly married couples to couples of similar circumstances. If a couple were on their second marriage, they would be attached to another couple who were having success with their second marriage. Couples that have a blended family would be connected to another successful blended family. What better way to grow your marriage than to spend time with another couple at the place where you desire to be? I believe this process could significantly reduce our current divorce rate, create more fulfilling marriages, and build connections outside Sunday's service.

What if we viewed counseling as a tune-up and not just for an emergency situation? If you purchase a new car, it comes with a preventative maintenance plan.

The operative word here is preventative.

The manufacturer has a scheduled maintenance plan for the upkeep of your new vehicle. At various intervals throughout the year, you are required to take the car to the dealership for service. In some cases, it could void the warranty if you don't take it to the dealer. The seller's intent is to prevent problems or catch issues *before* they surface.

What if we only took this same mindset with our marriages? Unfortunately, most people don't want to attend counseling unless there is a pressing issue. By this time the issue is so far left that it is extremely challenging to turn it right.

My wife and I attend workshops and participate in marriage ministry throughout the city. I admit, marriage is work, but if you invest in it, it will give a high return on your investment. Each time I attend a workshop, I pick up something I did not have before to aid in our success. Although I teach relationship workshops and counsel couples, I understand that I also need to be advised. If this is my profession and I get counseling for my marriage, you know I'm going to strongly recommend it for yours.

Will you go to counseling before and during your marriage? Why or why not?

Why is counseling (when nothing is wrong) so important?

What's the answer to staying married?

Not an Option

This is the oath my wife and I agreed to before the wedding:

Divorce is not an option.

So how do we begin to eliminate our chances of divorce? Both people must agree before and during the marriage that divorce is not an option because, and I'll say it again: *Divorce can't be an option!*

OUR OATH

Divorce is not an option.

We are one financial institution.

My partner is my next of kin.

We vow sexual exclusivity.

Love is a verb:
what we say must be demonstrated by what we do.

Being right is not always fruitful, but being fruitful is always right.

We will always seek to understand first, then to be understood.

Conflicts are inevitable, but we will handle them with respect for one another.

We will not go to bed mad.

We will always invest in our marriage: no investment, no return.

OUR GOAL: To have a lasting marriage worthy of emulation, and to be always looking to our heavenly Father for guidance.

Signed: Richard E. Hellen
Signed: Kim Y. Hellen

TEAM HELLEN

This oath is an extension of our vows and is a constant reminder of our commitment before God and man. Our oath has been framed and placed above our fireplace, and it's the first thing you see upon entry to our home. In case you have not noticed, it was also the inspiration for this book. People sometimes ask us why our oath is so visible. Anytime you want to accomplish something, and you are accountable to others for it coming to pass, you increase your chances of succeeding. Having our promise to each other made visible does two things:

1. It's a constant reminder of our commitment.

2. It makes us accountable to those who read it.

If you can agree to this, everything else will be minuscule. Let me point out what I assume to be obvious: If people are experiencing verbal or physical abuse, infidelity, etc., I'm not encouraging any of them to stay in that type of environment, but to get to a safe place and seek some professional guidance. However, when couples can agree on spiritual, emotional, financial, sexual and parental choices, it makes other issues minor and minimizes the chances of divorce.

Is divorce an option for your marriage?

What are you willing to sacrifice to ensure a lasting marriage?

Takeaways

- Your marriage can beat the odds if you use the right tools.
- Selfishness is the *number one* cause of divorce, and all other issues couples face are byproducts of selfishness.
- Adversity is normal.
- Stay true to your vows.
- Do marriage tune-ups regularly.

Notes

[1] https://www.psychologytoday.com/blog/the-intelligent-divorce/201202/the-high-failure-rate-second-and-third-marriages

CHAPTER 4

One Financial Institution

Money is not everything but it ranks right up there with oxygen.

~ Zig Ziglar

Depending on which report you read, it is safe to say that more than 50 percent of Americans are in debt to mortgages, student loans, car loans, and credit card debt. We are inundated with commercials showcasing nice cars, clothing, furniture, and everything that appeals to our tastes. The always lingering question is why we can't have some of the finer things in life and live like the Smiths or Joneses. One thing that is not always evident is that we usually have no idea about the Smiths' or Joneses' financial situation. There is nothing wrong with having the better things in life; it's what we are willing to sacrifice to have them. Having the finer things in life should not cause us to live check to check, or as my mother would say, have to rob Peter to pay Paul. Sometimes we have to ask if money is the issue or if there is an underlying issue that needs addressing.

Is a Deeper Issue Lingering?

One day an NBA player and his father were discussing the number of vehicles parked in his driveway—ten cars and five trucks. As his father looked at this excess, he said: "You have all of these vehicles, but you only have one a**." His father was not questioning whether or not his son could afford his lifestyle, but why he needed to live with so much excess. He was wondering who he was trying to impress, or if he was overcompensating for his insecurities.

> *Does having nice things compensate for some of your insecurities?*
>
> *Would you rather be known for what you have or who you have become?*

Looking Good on the Outside but Miserable on the Inside

One of my friends grew up poor and vowed he would do much better for his family. He managed to marry a very educated woman who also came from poor and humble beginnings. Shortly after their marriage, he landed an excellent sales job, and life could not have been better. After all, he had a beautiful wife, no kids, and dual incomes. It appeared his prayer for a better life for his family was answered.

A few years later they had children, which added a different dynamic to the relationship. When the children became of age, he placed them in private schools so they could receive the finest education. As fate would have it, they found a nice middle-class home about five miles from the children's school. He said he often thought he was dreaming.

From the outside looking in, they had the epitome of a life to be envied. Beautiful home, children in private schools, and good jobs. The only problem was that inside this beautiful home were two broke and frustrated people. They had no savings, no money for a rainy day, and no monies for the children's college. Each time he got paid, he was paying the bills from the previous week. Their financial situation began to cause stress in their marriage and it affected their health.

No vision + no plan = stress and frustration

At some point, being wise must override looking good to impress people we don't know—people who do not care about our well-being. The goal is not to live within our means but below our means. This takes having a vision for our finances and the discipline to execute it.

"If you make money your god, it will plague you like the devil." ~ Anonymous proverb, Select Proverbs of All Nations *(1824)*

Do you live above, below, or within your means?

Are you living to impress others?

How long can you survive if one or both parties lost their jobs?

Do you live on one income or two?

What are your short-term goals?

Do you have an emergency fund?

Do you have a benevolence fund?

Do you have a college fund for the children?

As a young man, I watched my mother manage the finances, and what she did with them was nothing short of a miracle. My father didn't make a significant amount of money, but my mom knew how to make a dollar stretch. There was never a time when our lights were off or food was not in the kitchen. I can never recall going hungry or having to ask neighbors or family for food. What was her secret? My mother did two things well: she lived within her means, and she was disciplined. I witnessed this at a young age, and my mom's financial practices have influenced my financial behavior. My goal is to always live under and never above my income. I have refused to allow something I can purchase to ever own me or define who I am. Many people in our society like to be identified by what they have instead of who they are, and as a result, are head over heels in debt.

Are you defined by your character or things?

Are you able to distinguish your needs from your wants? What is the difference?

Financial Agreement

"Too many people spend money they earn to buy things they don't want, to impress people that they don't like." ~ Will Rogers

"For the love of money is the root of all evil: which while some coveted after, they have erred from the faith, and pierced themselves through with many sorrows" (1 Timothy 6:10). This Scripture is often quoted, but most people leave out "the love of" part. Money is not evil, but the love of money is. If you think money is evil, please e-mail me and I'll give you my bank routing information.

Money is often the great divide in relationships. Money is not everything, but according to Cicero, a Roman politician and lawyer, being frugal includes all the other virtues. Before marriage, many couples never discuss finances in totality.

Questions such as:

- Will we pay our bills on time?
- How much money will we give to our local religious establishment or church?
- What will be the protocol for people borrowing money from us?
- What will be our protocol for borrowing money from lending institutions?

- Will we make all financial decisions together?
- Will our monies be separate or together?
- Will we save?
- How much money will we invest?

If not discussed, all of these issues can cause turmoil that leads to emotional and physical separation. If your money is *your* money and his money is *his* money, you will never become one.

Before marriage, my wife and I sat down and discussed these questions and other perspectives on finances. We wanted to operate as one united front. Our first goal was to move from talking about her and my money to referring to it as *our* money. I am often amazed when I hear couples have separate bank accounts. Why would you do that? Are you attempting to hide your actions to keep from being accountable? When money is kept separate from each other, it creates isolation, which is the first sign of marital destruction. Instead of having an *us* and *our* marriage, they have an *I* and *mine* marriage. Just for the record, *I* and *mine* never create a successful union. "'For this cause shall a man leave father and mother, and shall cleave to his wife: and they twain shall be one flesh?'" (Matthew 19:5). This means we are also meant to become one with our finances, along with every other aspect of our marriages.

My wife and I have several bank accounts, but we are both listed on all accounts. At any time, either one of us could take out all the money and leave the other person destitute. What is the point of getting married if you don't trust each other? When you enter marriage with a separatist mentality, you're divorced before you get married. If you decide to move forward with the marriage, it will only be on paper and not in the heart. It is impossible to have a successful marriage or relationship that's not based upon trust. "This people draweth nigh unto me with their mouth, and honoureth me with their lips; but their heart is far from me" (Matthew 15:8).

Will our money be in one account or two?

Will each of our names be on all the accounts?

How much debt will we incur?

Will we borrow or pay cash for everything?

Will we rent or buy a home? If buying, how long will we get financing for, and why?

How much money will we allot for church?

What will be our policy on family members and friends borrowing money?

Discussing and unifying decisions on how monies will be distributed is necessary for the health of the marriage. This will keep fighting over money to a minimum, and sometimes eliminate fighting over monies altogether. Word to the wise: However you decide to allocate your funds, make sure you discuss why and how it's advantageous to the marriage. Do you want separate accounts, or will your accounts be together? Why or why not? Lead your finances with purpose so your finances are not leading you.

Talk about Finances before Marriage

From the beginning of our marriage, we set up several bank accounts. We have a primary checking, two personal accounts, one business account, and one emergency fund. We both have access to all the accounts with full disclosure and trust. We discuss the allocation of all monies and make every financial decision as a *team.* Working as a team is imperative for a successful marriage, and especially critical in the financial department. We know that one bad financial decision could be the difference between living in our own home or having to move in with our parents or friends, and sometimes, children.

I have mentioned the words *team* and *partnership* a few times throughout the book. For me, this is the key ingredient in every aspect of our marriage. Show me a couple who operate as a team, and I'll show you a couple with an exceptional marriage. Show me a couple who operate independently of one another, and I'll introduce you to misery. When talking about being a team, I envision two people working together for a common goal and willing to make the necessary sacrifices for its obtainment. No better place to start operating as a team than with our finances.

When one or both parties have separate accounts, it usually constitutes having a different agenda. Growing up, my elders would always encourage me to have a separate account unbeknownst to my wife. Their rationale was I'd never know what was going to happen and I'd need a backup plan. I never understood that, even as a naïve young man. The only way marriage can succeed is if it is based upon trust. If you are contemplating marriage with someone you don't trust, you are already divorced.

Accountability

Because our money is together, I am more conscious about my spending. This makes me accountable to my spouse for my spending habits. The question I often ask couples is, Does keeping money separate bring them closer or does it create a greater divide in their marriage? In almost all cases, it doesn't create a closer union, because the less you communicate, the further you grow apart. If you are considering getting married and someone has a different financial plan that does not involve unity, it might be best to consider staying single. If you are already married but not united financially, I recommend counseling or finding someone to place on your board of directors (see chapter 12) for guidance.

Couples fight over money more than they fight over anything else in marriage, so I want to conclude with two critical points:

> Finances have to be approached with a team mindset and not a selfish, individual perspective.
> Financial decisions have to be made dependent on how their consequences will affect the marriage long term.

I am unwilling to make a large purchase unbeknownst to my spouse just because it's something I desire (selfishness). I also must consider how this decision will affect our long-term financial plans.

One of our goals is to pay off our home. We once contemplated purchasing a new home, but that decision was not good for us long term. Our house will be paid for in a few years, and if we buy another home, that gives us a mortgage payment into retirement. This approach caused us to take looking for a new home off the table and allowed us to make an informed decision as a *team.*

Takeaways

- Control your money rather than letting money, or the lack of it, control you.
- Live within your means.
- Set up a lifelong financial agreement with your spouse.
- Stay accountable to each other re spending.

CHAPTER 5

Your Spouse Comes First

If your kids, parents, and siblings come before your spouse, they're the ones ruling your household.

Out of all the chapters in this book, this chapter will probably present the biggest challenge for some marriages, and for others, it will be confirmation. What I'm about to share might be against what most of you believe, and some may disagree, and that's okay. Many of the things I'm writing about go against what we have been taught, as well as what we have seen. Most of our lives, we have been exposed to outside-in versus inside-out principles. Outside principles focus on *what* we are doing, whereas inside principles focus on *why* we are doing them. My goal is to get us to speak the same language by starting with *why* (our purpose) and not *what.* Let's take a closer look.

If you don't know your why, you will always have disagreements about your what and your how. If you understand your why, your what and how just gained clarity.

The Golden Circle

Start with Your Purpose

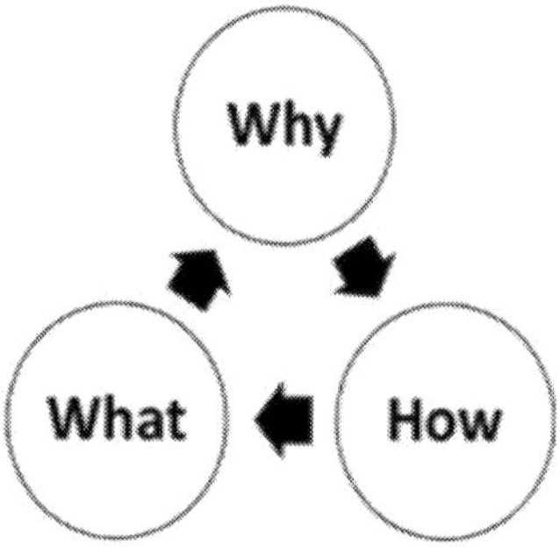

WHY = your purpose

WHAT = your products or services

HOW = your processes

My first experience with the above diagram was when I watched Simon Sinek in a TED Talk entitled "Start with WHY." His concept was not a new concept, but he codified the process. Sinek explained that most people and organizations approach situations from what is clear (what) and work their way up to what might not be so apparent (why). It is easier to start with *what* we are doing and *how* we are going to do it than to define *why* we are doing it. Almost all of us know *what* we are doing, but we gain clarity when we understand *why* we are doing it. *Why* denotes our cause, belief, or purpose, and is the engine that drives the relationship. Team Hellen's *why:* We desire a lasting marriage worthy of emulation, and to always look to our heavenly Father, as we are fully conscious of where our guidance will

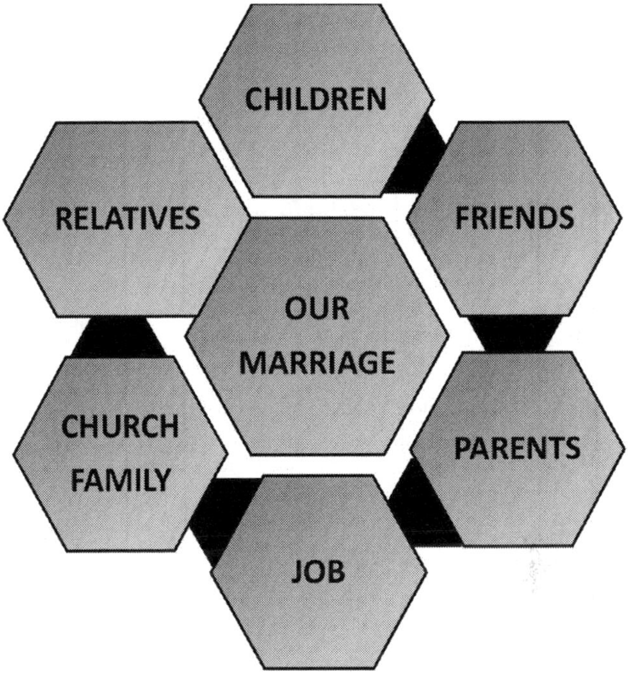

come from. We desire a marriage that's a reflection of our Savior.

> *We will not let anything outside our marriage negatively affect our marriage and our purpose. That means ANYTHING.*

The hexagon in the center represents our marriage driven by our *why,* and the smaller hexagons symbolize outside influences. The challenge with the outside influences is that they are usually from those we love, such as our parents, children, friends, and our religious family. If you and your spouse planned a date night and the neighbor called and asked if you could babysit, you might not have a hard time saying no. On the other hand, if it is your mother, you might give babysitting more consideration. This is not to say that you won't sometimes forgo your plans to serve someone else. I'm trying to make you conscious of what you let in your circle, how often you let things in your circle, and for what reason. Whoever and whatever you let into your circle will influence your marriage. This influence could be positive or negative, but rest assured, your relationship will be influenced. You have to exercise wisdom regarding what gets in and what goes out. Although every situation and circumstance will be different, just be reminded that your spouse is your next of kin, and the only way your marriage succeeds is when your spouse comes first.

The First Woman I loved

Several years ago, my mother called letting me know that she needed some financial assistance. My mom was a homemaker, and when my father passed, there was not a surplus of monies. With such a strain, all it took was one small setback to put her finances in ruins. If you are similar to me, I don't want to see my mother in need of anything. After all, this is the woman who sacrificed her dreams to ensure that I had the opportunity to pursue mine. There is no way I'm going to let her do without, even if it means I have to sacrifice something. I find one of the greatest joys in life is having the ability to give back to something or someone that gave to me. I call this "feeding what has fed you."

After my mother explained her concerns, I told her her financial problem should not be an issue but that I'd speak with Kim first and call her back. I had no doubt my wife would be in agreement; however, I never want my spouse to believe she has no input because it's my mom, or that she has to be second in any situation. The day I said I do, my wife became my (first) priority. If I decide to do anything without her consent, we are not operating as a team but as separate and distinct singles. This does not mean that my mother's issues were not a concern; I just never want to create other concerns by working independently of my spouse. The world has enough marriages that operate with independence, but successful marriages consist of couples who work with interdependence. My spouse is my next of kin.

Is your spouse your first priority, and where is everyone else in the pecking order?

Does your spouse know where he or she is in the pecking order?

Who or what do you choose over your spouse?

Nothing happens outside our household that's not first discussed within, because the sanctity and health of our marriage is at stake if we even consider not discussing it. That means that even if one of my family members calls and is need of our immediate assistance, my wife has to approve. If an issue is not discussed, this could easily make my spouse feel overlooked and not valued. In simplistic terms, keep the main thing the main thing, which builds a healthy marriage. Communication should always be open, and nothing outside the home should ever cause friction within. When we collaborate and things go awry, the team takes the blame; however, when we make decisions solo and things go awry, we can find ourselves on an island by ourselves.

Our Basic Needs

It's no secret that men and women are different regarding their needs for acceptance within the relationship. Not knowing and understanding these differences can further complicate the relationship. Once we understand each other's basic needs, it brings lucidity to what was once ambiguous. Relationships never exist without conflict; however, understanding these requirements minimizes some of the pressure.

WOMEN'S PRIMARY NEEDS

1. Security
2. Open and honest communication
3. Affection
4. Leadership

MEN'S PRIMARY NEEDS

1. Honor
2. Sex
3. Friendship
4. Support

A woman's primary need is usually *security*, and her second need is *open and honest communication.* If I make a decision without Kim's input, I violate her primary and secondary basic needs. She will feel insecure and be frustrated that I didn't inform her about the decision. Coming in second is sometimes okay in sports, but it's unacceptable in marriage. Maybe the first time someone needed help, it was my mother, but what about when it's my sibling or friends? At what point do I inform Kim about my intentions? Security is just like trust: it takes years to build, but with one wrong decision, it could be destroyed. Whenever I speak to my spouse, I have to learn to talk in her language of security, because any other language will create a disconnection.

It is imperative that we learn and know each other's primary needs to keep us out of the penalty box. If you are not familiar with the penalty box, it is a sitting area for people who have committed some offense during an ice hockey or rugby game. Men often refer to this as the doghouse.

RESPECT FOR MEN

If the wife is making decisions without the husband's input, he can feel dishonored as the leader of the household. A man's primary need is respect. This might be hard to conceive, but most men desire respect and honor above sex. When we are disrespected, it causes severe dissension, and sometimes emotional or physical abandonment. The man has already left home; it just has not manifested yet.

My First Priority

What I did with my mom was probably contrary to how many people would have handled the situation, because we believe we are obligated to assist our parents. I can't say I don't understand; however, if not careful, those we love can take advantage of us and leave our spouses feeling like outsiders. These actions may not be done deliberately, but it happens nonetheless. Your wife begins to shut down, and you have no idea as to the cause of her isolation—because if it is your mother you helped, your wife might be reluctant to share her concerns. She doesn't want to appear to be lacking compassion about your mom's situation.

SO LET'S GET TO THE POINT

What is meant by my spouse being my next of kin? My wife is my first priority, and she is not competing with my children, parents, sibling, friends, church, or occupation. Everything is communicated with my spouse so that we are always operating as one, and so those we love will witness our oneness. If this is not understood, people can, and will, drive a wedge in your relationship. This atrocity is not the fault of outside influences, but of the people who allow this infiltration into their relationship. What we tolerate is what we teach.

"And Adam said, this is now bone of my bones, and flesh of my flesh: she shall be called Woman because she was taken out of Man. Therefore shall a man leave his father and his mother, and shall cleave unto his wife: and they shall be one flesh" (Genesis 2:23–24). We refer to this as *leave and cleave.* This can't just be a popular Bible verse; it has to become our reality if our goal is to succeed in marriage. My wife is my next of kin.

Do you and your partner operate as one?

Can your parents divide you and your spouse? How do they accomplish it?

Parental Agreement

OPERATING AS ONE BEFORE AND AFTER THE MARRIAGE

One of the greatest gifts we can give our children is the modeling of a healthy marriage that places the marriage first. Children are self-centered, which is an innate behavior. From the womb, it is all about them, and they have little concern for what types of sacrifices are necessary to accommodate their wants and needs. Parents are often not conscious that this selfishness can drive a wedge in their marriage and create hardship, so parents must be in agreement regarding how they will parent to prevent and minimize disruption in the relationship. When children see that parents are not in agreement, they will exploit, divide, and conquer for personal gain. Parents will complain and blame the children for this commotion, but the children are a reflection of the culture the parents have created. Creating the culture in the home begins with the parents and not the children. If we blame the children, we have just abdicated our leadership role as parents.

Very seldom do I hear people talking about management or leadership regarding parenting. These are terms used quite frequently in the marketplace and not in the home. Let's take a closer look at the difference between management and leadership, because knowing the difference makes the difference. Management looks at maintaining and monitoring (the now), whereas leadership looks at the same thing but focuses on how the now will influence tomorrow. Management is at its best when things stay the same, whereas leadership focuses on creating change and facilitating growth.

Management and Leadership Displayed in the Home

When our son was sixteen, my wife and I agreed to purchase him a 1992 Honda Accord Ex for his first car. It wasn't that we couldn't have afforded a newer model, but a teachable moment was in the works. As we discussed this purchase, we agreed that the car needed to come with some clear expectations and responsibilities: He couldn't drive his car until he had learned how to change the tires and oil, listen for unusual noises, and learn some basic maintenance skills. If at any time I checked the car and saw these issues were being neglected, we would take his keys for a week. As leaders of the household, we expected all maintenance on the car to be up to date at all times.

Our children are a temporary assignment, and we must prepare them for the day they will leave the nest. If we raise them as if they are always going to be with us, they will. We purchased the car for our son to satisfy an immediate need (management), but we were preparing him for tomorrow by laying down our clear expectations for driving (leadership). Our son was in a band, and it had become extremely time-consuming trying to accommodate his schedule. Teaching him how to drive and getting him a car was a blessing for all parties.

Too frequently we give our children things that require no responsibility or sacrifice on their part. Unbeknownst to us, we create children with a sense of entitlement and a lack of appreciation. This character flaw will resurface later in their relationships, marriages, and work ethic. If what's received comes with no sacrifice or responsibility, it will have no perceived value.

When our son graduated high school in 2012, he joined the United States Air Force. When he arrived at his first duty station, his priority was to purchase his first vehicle. He was so proud, because he did everything without any assistance from us. A few months after his arrival at his new duty station, we paid him a visit. When we arrived, I must say I was pleased with the cleanliness of his vehicle, but more delighted that he was still checking the oil and keeping up with the basic maintenance on it. In life there are no guarantees; however, if we love, teach, and train our children, we increase their chances of succeeding and being responsible adults.

Although I led the charge, my wife and I agreed that buying our son that car was best for our son's long-term success (leadership). Children need to see that both parents are on the same team and in total agreement on every decision. Even if we disagree, we go behind closed doors and discuss the situation. When our decision has concluded, we show one unified front. When children see how their parents operate, it lays the foundation for how they will conduct themselves in their future relationships.

Blended Families

A blended family consists of children from a previous marriage or relationship. More than 40 percent of marriages consist of step couples.[1] This challenging dynamic creates a much higher chance of divorce than a nuclear family does.

Blending means to combine separate parts in such a way that the individual parts can no longer be distinguished. During workshops, I take red and blue Kool-Aid® to represent two families with separate children. I have a couple leave the room while the two colors are mixed. Once the couple comes back into the room, I ask what color they see. Every time, the couple states they see purple Kool-Aid. This is the color you get when you combine red and blue. The couple has no idea that we combined two separate colors because all they see is one color. If the child or other people can easily tell that the family is a mix of two previous marriages, it's the first sign of a dysfunctional relationship. The biggest problem with combined families is that they might never become blended.

Is it obvious that you are a combination of two families with separate children?

If so, what can you do to change that?

You Can't Marry Without Marrying the Children

If you are not ready to marry the children, you are not ready for marriage. It's a package deal. Your conversation is a good indicator of how much of the entire package you have accepted. When men say they have one child and their wife/girlfriend/fiancée has two kids, they are not ready. The Bible states, "The two will become one flesh. So they are no longer two, but one flesh" (Mark 10:8 NIV). I refer to this as the law of possession, which states we share everything as one, even our children. If he can't see the children as his and she's not willing to share her kids, the marriage will not succeed and the children will be negatively affected.

Some men who understand the children come with the package will often ask the children (when appropriate) if it is okay to marry their mother. If she has daughters, he sometimes gives them each a ring to show his commitment to them and their mother. It's not hard to see how this man would have a buy in with the children before the ceremony and not have to wait to seek their acceptance. If the children feel as if they are included instead of excluded, he will not have to leverage their support. People support what they help create or support a decision when they were asked for their input. This approach is robust, and a game changer for the marriage from the beginning. Marry the children or don't marry the woman, because it should be a package deal.

The Challenge

In blended families, people have children first and then become a couple, whereas in a nuclear family the couple comes first followed by the children. Blended families start the marriage relationship sharing their time, resources, and monies with the children and experiencing little time for themselves. Instead of getting to know one another and experiencing martial bless, their time is often delegated to the children. This dynamic creates many challenges, and if the couple are not hypersensitive to all the varying needs, it will cause the demise of the marriage.

Being in agreement in a nuclear family is imperative; however, in a blended family, it's like oxygen. Couples have to show a united front at all times, and the children need to see all decisions being made together. Unity will assist in resolving inequity, which is one of blended families' most pressing issues. If either parent shows preference to his or her children, it will cause a separate and slow death of the marriage. One of the systems my wife and I implemented was to create situations where my daughter had to come to me for certain things. One of my roles was overseeing our finances, so when my daughter wanted a new phone, she would have to come to me. This created intentional interaction between me and my nonbiological child. If there is no type of intervention like this, the nonbiological child will usually defer to the biological parent. This is particularly the case at the beginning of the relationship.

> *If there has to be a bad parent, it must be the biological parent.*

If one or both parties are not ready to share the kids, it is often best to sacrifice your needs and desires for the emotional well-being of the children. Some couples wait on marriage until after the children are in college or the workforce and no longer living in the home.

Take special consideration when the kids are older, because you will face a different set of challenges then. If you meet someone and the children are under two years of age, you can have a tremendous influence on their lives. On the other hand, if you meet someone and the children are eight years old or older, it can present significant challenges, because their character, habits, and traits are already established and are sometimes harder to influence. Proceed with caution.

For all blended families to succeed, both parties have to be on the same team, going in the same direction, making all decisions together, with the best interest of the family in mind. They have to move from a *me* perspective to an *us* perspective.

Discipline to Consider before Marriage in Blended Families

> *"It is much easier to build strong children than to repair broken men." ~ Frederick Douglass*

Spare the rod and you will surely spoil the child. This doesn't mean children need corporal punishment, but they do need and want some form of discipline. In blended families, the discipline has to stem from the biological parent and be supported by the nonbiological parent. At the beginning of the relationship, the nonbiological parent may have little or no influence on the children. If you have no influence, you are disciplining the child based upon your position in the household. It's always best to let the discipline stem from the biological parent until influence has been established. However, if you are that parent that went into the relationship understanding that it's a package deal, you may already have influence. Still, proceed with caution.

How will we parent together?

How will we show unification in front of the children and why?

If blended, who will initiate the discipline and why?

If blended, how do we make sure things are equitable?

What role will the nonbiological parent have regarding parenting the children?

Are the children your children or our children, and how is that demonstrated?

If blended, will a relationship be established with the other parent? Why or why not?

What is the difference between managing your children versus leading them?

Seven Steps to Raising Emotionally Healthy Children

I can't guarantee these steps will offer you success with your parenting, but I can assure you that if they are not implemented, you will have some severe parenting challenges. This are the seven things I believe that all children need:

UNCONDITIONAL LOVE

> Love for them cannot be based upon what they do or who they become. We love them just because they are our children.

CLEAR EXPECTATIONS

> Whatever we expect from them needs to be clear, and preferably written down for clarity. Also, what they

can expect from us needs to be written down, because accountability works best when both parties are accountable to one another.

STRUCTURE OR SYSTEM

Our children need some structured systems because the world we live in operates through systems. If they don't have structure, they will struggle with structure in school and work.

DISCIPLINE

Children need and want discipline. Our children question our love for them when we refrain from some form of discipline.

REWARDS

What we desire has to be repeated, recognized, and rewarded. If not recognized or rewarded, the good behavior you want will cease.

OUR TIME

If you lose money, you can recoup your losses; however, you can't recoup your time. Our children need our money, but they are crying for our time.

After seven-year-old Lisa's father made it home from work, she asked him how much he made an hour. Her father told her he made one hundred dollars, but wanted to know why, so she said she needed to borrow fifty dollars. Frustrated, he yelled at her and sent her to her room. After feeling bad, he went to her room and apologized for his tone. He asked why she needed fifty dollars, and she told him she had

> managed to save fifty dollars and needed an additional fifty dollars to buy an hour of his time.

MODEL

> Everyone is a model. If we are not modeling what we are teaching, we are showing something else. If what we teach is not what we live, what we teach will have no real value. Our influence will be based upon what we model. This will dictate whether or not we lead our children by our position or our disposition.

Our position forces our children to follow because we are their parents, while our disposition influences them to follow because of our character.

> One Wednesday afternoon, Pastor Carter was sitting in his office contemplating how he was going to resolve several new issues in his church. After careful consideration and hours of frustration, he headed home for dinner with his wife and son. As they were sitting at the table, the doorbell rang. Before his wife answered the door, she asked her husband, "If it's for you, are you home?" The pastor replied, "Tell them I'm not here because I've had a long tiring day." As she opened the door, she stated: "My husband is not home. Can I take a message?"
>
> The pastor then asked his son to say grace. His son prayed, "God, thank you for the food and the hands that prepared it, and can you help my parents learn to be honest."

Before and during the marriage, if couples can agree on their spiritual, emotional, financial, sexual, and parental foundations, it increases their chances of experiencing success.

Our Children Are Our Greatest Challenge

The way you were raised will usually dictate the way you will raise your children. Although I use the word "raise" because it is common, I'm a firm believer that we raise cattle but lead our children. If you came from an affluent home, you might feel obligated to spoil your children. Sometimes those of us whose parents were not wealthy have a tendency to also attempt to spoil our kids, even if we don't have the resources to do so. Parents that don't have a father for their children often raise children feeling guilty, and they allow them to grow up without consequences. All of these situations will affect our parenting styles.

Keep in mind that how we respond to various situations will depend mostly on what we were exposed to growing up. Sometimes we are not responding to the situation in front of us but things we have experienced that are behind us. It doesn't matter how hard we try, our past always finds a way of entering our present.

Back to the action:

A MOTHER'S LOVE

Sandra's nineteen-year-old son, Jamal, asked to borrow the car to go to his friend's party. He said the party would end at midnight and that he should be home by 11:30 p.m. Sandra generally conferred with her husband on these decisions, but her husband was out of town on business. Sandra gave Jamal a few rules and informed him not to miss his midnight curfew. Excited, Jamal headed to the party.

While at the party, Jamal ran into some of his old high school friends. They were taking shots of tequila and seeing who could drink the most without passing out. Not wanting to be left out, Jamal joined in on the fun for about ten minutes, after which he'd had about as much as his body could take. He attempted to absorb some of the alcohol by eating some chicken and drinking plenty of water.

At about 11 p.m., Jamal decided he'd had enough fun and it was time for him to head home. As he drove home, he fell asleep, and the car veered off the road and hit a pole, which rendered him unconscious. Luckily, the driver behind him called the police, and the EMS arrived within minutes. They took him to the hospital and tested his blood alcohol level, which was twice the legal limit. After being released from the hospital, he was taken to the county jail. As soon as Jamal was able to make his first phone call, he called his mother, who immediately bailed him out on a $20,000 bond.

REVIEW

Should Sandra have contacted her husband before giving Jamal the keys?

Did it help or hurt Jamal by bailing him out of his situation so quickly?

Could this add some tension to Sandra's marriage?

Did Jamal see them operate as one or as individuals?

Could this event make Jamal think he could divide and conquer his parents in future?

Which of Sandra's husband's basic needs might Sandra have violated?

Men and women have different basic needs, but all those needs on the list are important to all of us. In the above story, Sandra was not open in her communication with her husband.

Although a woman's second basic need is open and honest communication, make no mistake, men want the same thing. Sandra's husband could easily have felt disrespected because nothing was communicated, and he found out about the drinking, the accident, jail, and the bail money after all the decisions had been made.

When decisions are made together, we create a team culture, whereas when decisions are made separately, we form a self-centered culture in the home. Marriages can't sustain themselves if the culture is self-centered. The scenario above is all too common—decisions are made and there is no collaboration between parties. When we men ask our wives for their inputs on decisions, it states we value and appreciate them. If we fail to ask for their insight, we could be unconsciously sending a message that we don't value them or their input. However, when we agree that our wives are our next of kin, we don't think twice about getting their input. We need to ensure our spouses know their position in the relationship. Life-changing decisions could be life changing for the marriage if they are not made collaboratively.

My spouse is my first priority and my next of kin.

Takeaways

- Your spouse should be your first priority. Make your spouse your first reason for choosing anything.
- Security and respect go hand in hand.
- The children should never come before your spouse, because one day they are going to leave the home.
- Understand each other's basic needs.
- If the children are your first priority, the inmates are running the asylum.

Notes

[1] http://www.myfamilymedallion.com/blog/ultimate-stepfamily-blended-family-statistics-guide

CHAPTER 6

We Vow Sexual Exclusivity

Some things are better than sex, and some are worse, but there's nothing exactly like it. ~ *W. C. Fields*

Between 30–60 percent of all marriages will engage in infidelity at some point during the relationship;[1] however, this is a very conservative figure. Based on the couples I have encountered and counseled over the years, those numbers are quite generous.

Infidelity is so commonplace in our society that if you are faithful to your spouse, you might be considered abnormal. Over the last several years, many clergymen have been caught in various sex scandals and affairs. After being exposed, they apologized and within a few weeks, back to the pulpit they went. I am not implying that pastors don't deserve forgiveness or a second chance, because we all need forgiveness. My concern is not forgiveness—the people who have a hard time forgiving have lost sight that the Savior on the cross forgave them—but that our expectations of self and others have dwindled.

Sexual Agreement

> *"Sex is the most fun you can have without laughing." ~ Woody Allen*

According to Maslow's Hierarchy of Needs, love and belonging (sex and intimacy) are not an option but a necessity for fulfillment.

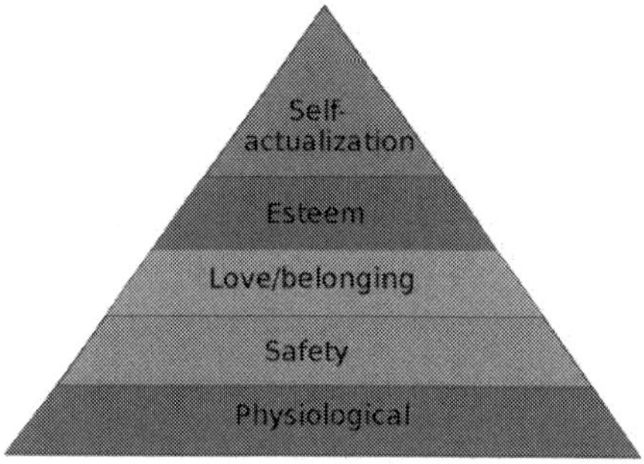

By FireflySixtySeven[2]

No one seems comfortable talking about sex, yet most people can't wait until their next sexual encounter. Men have been known to walk, ride, and/or swim for miles to have their sexual needs fulfilled. Sex is like a drug—once you experience it, you keep coming back to try to duplicate the last experience. Each day people risk losing their families, children, and sometimes their occupation for sex. On second thought, sex might be stronger than drugs.

If two people are to marry and be faithful to one another for life, sex is something that must be discussed. This is a conversation that can't be sugarcoated or taken lightly. Unsatisfied sexual needs can lead to infidelity and emotional abandonment. Therefore, before and after the wedding, couples can't be afraid to express their sexual concerns.

Paul wrote: "The wife does not have authority over her own body but yields it to her husband. In the same way, the husband does not have authority over his own body but yields it to his wife. Do not deprive each other except perhaps by mutual consent and for a time, so that you may devote yourselves to prayer. Then come together again so that Satan will not tempt you because of your lack of self-control" (1 Corinthians 7:4–5 NIV). The day we get married, we lose the authority of our bodies. My body belongs to her and her body belongs to me. However, our bodies are for each other's use and not abuse. Men have the greater need for sex and women have the gift of sex. When these two come together of one accord, sex goes to an entirely different level.

SOME OF OUR GROUND RULES

If my wife is sick, my goal is to help her heal, not satisfy my sexual desire. If I were to make my desire supersede her need for healing, she would still be intimate with me, but I'd be indicating that my desires were more important to me than her health. This demonstration of selfishness could have severe consequences on the relationship and our future sexual relations. The goal for success in marriage is selflessness and not selfishness, so apart from some illness, we never turn each other away sexually.

SEX SHOULD NEVER BE USED AS A WEAPON

My wife and I agreed to never use sex as a weapon or to refrain from meeting each other's sexual needs. If we chose to abstain from sex based upon some temporary emotion, that would make sex in our marriage conditional. I never want my wife to leave home and not have her sexual needs met. Nor do I want to refrain from sex because I want to get even with my spouse. Remember, no part of our relationship is about winning but about understanding one another. Winning and losing is for sports but has no place in marriage, but it often shows its ugly face during a divorce.

If I choose to wait until I'm in the mood for sex, my spouse could go days or weeks without being fulfilled. It doesn't matter if I'm mad or tired, my desire is still to satisfy her sexually. Sometimes having sex during those difficult times opens the door for deeper communication and greater sex. If we are committed to satisfying one another sexually, it becomes difficult for people outside our home to get our attention, let alone get us in their bedrooms. Therefore, if you don't feel like doing it, do it anyway, and I guarantee you'll feel like doing it.

Can we have sex if we are mad?

What is off limits sexually?

How often can we have sex?

What positions are off limits?

Is the bedroom undefiled?

WHATEVER IT TAKES TO SATISFY HER

The apostle Saul stated "To the weak, I became weak that I might win the weak. I have become all things to all people that I might save some (1 Corinthians 9:22 NIV). When our bedroom door closes, I might become an exotic male dancer, electrician, carpenter, plumber, or whatever she needs to ensure satisfaction, and sometimes this requires a little creativity.

If we desire a lifetime of sexual fulfillment, it's going to take a lifetime of creativity. The minute we stop investing is the moment our minds begin to start wandering. Sometimes men go outside the home to fulfill some fantasy and not understand that their fantasy is lying next to them. Be creative at home, because the grass is not greener on the other side; it's only green where it's being watered.

OUR FIVE LOVE LANGUAGES

Physical touch
Words of affirmation
Gifts
Acts of service
Quality time

How We Differ

MEN

For men, sex is physical, and it doesn't take much for us to become stimulated or to satisfy us sexually. Whenever I conduct a workshop, 90 percent of all men's love language is "physical touch" and "words of affirmation." whereas with women, it's never that consistent. If a woman wants to make her man feel special, all she needs to do to communicate love is compliment him in public (affirmation) and later that night come on to him sexually (physical touch). It's that simple for most men. Boost our egos and cater to our libido, and we are the happiest people on earth.

What are his primary and secondary love languages?

1.

2.

WOMEN

Unfortunately, it is not this simple when it comes to women. When I ask women about their primary love languages, their answers vary significantly. If a woman's primary love language is not physical touch, we can't approach her speaking our language. When we learn to speak a woman's love language, it creates a connection and increases the chance for deeper intimacy.

What's her primary and secondary love language?

1.

2.

Whereas sex for men is physical, it is more emotional for women. Men have to understand that lovemaking begins between a woman's temples before they get in the bedroom. Stimulate her emotionally or she will not be ready to receive you sexually. Just remember, stimulation from above before stimulation below.

When most men think of foreplay, they only consider things they do in the bedroom. Since sex for women is emotional, foreplay should take place more often outside the bedroom than inside. The husband might give his wife an intimate hug before work, sexy text messages, flowers, and other things to get the emotional juices flowing before physical intimacy. If this sounds like work, it is. Successful relationships begin with two people always seeking ways to add value to one another. This is the line of demarcation between couples having an average sex life to couples having an exceptional sex life. Intentionality means everything.

I learned years ago that when we help people get what they want, those same people will help us get what we want. The more planting we do, the greater the harvest. If we are unwilling to invest the time, we will not generate the desired return. Every man yearns for a wife who is enthusiastic about coming together sexually; we just can't forget some of her excitement will come from what we have invested.

Bob, who had been married for twenty years, told Ralph that he was considering having an affair with Susan. Bob and Susan worked for the same engineering firm and had worked together on several projects. Bob said his sex life with his wife had become stale, and he needed some excitement. Ralph, who was also married, said Susan was beautiful, and he would seize any opportunity to wake up next to her as well.

It's no coincidence that Bob confided in Ralph about his intentions of infidelity; he knew they shared the same values.

Parents tell their children to be careful about the kids they associate with, because parents know their children will turn out like the company they keep. At what point in our lives is this not true? Couples who are serious about success find other couples who will hold them accountable.

IS IT POSSIBLE?

With man, some things are possible. With God, *all* things are possible. A relationship with God in its center changes everything in the marriage. We no longer depend on ourselves and each other—we are dependent upon God for direction and guidance. If we place our faith in ourselves and not in God, being faithful becomes impossible; but when we make God our north star, we understand that being unfaithful to our spouses means we are unfaithful to him.

WHERE INFIDELITY BEGINS

The apostle Paul wrote "Do not deprive each other except perhaps by mutual consent and for a time, so that you may devote yourselves to prayer. Then come together again so that Satan will not tempt you because of your lack of self-control" (1 Corinthians 7:5 NIV). When you deprive your spouse, you're denying him or her part of yourself. Husbands and wives should not deny each other sexually, which is true. Men are physical, and sex is the man's second primary need, and words of affirmation are most men's love language. Women need sex as well, but for women, sex is more emotional than physical. A woman's primary need is security, and her second need is open and honest communication. Whenever our love language or basic needs go unmet, it makes going outside our marriage more enticing; however, this in no way justifies our actions.

For the following example, let's say the woman's primary love language is words of affirmation and her second is physical touch.

HARVEY'S STORY

Harvey goes to a coffee shop for lunch and he notices a lady sitting next to him. They begin to pass a few pleasantries and quickly notice they have a few things in common. She tells him her name is Rhonda, and she is from New York. As they are talking, she compliments him on his beautiful smile and his athletic build. She is speaking his love language right into his heart. For the first time in years, he feels wanted and appreciated. He begins to blush from ear to ear but unfortunately has to cut the conversation short because of work.

The next day he goes back to the same coffee shop, quickly scans the room, and pays for his coffee. Rhonda walks through the door. They both sit at the same table, and Rhonda notices how well his shirt is fitting his body. She asks how often he works out and if he played football in college. Feeling rejuvenated, he goes down memory lane, from high school to his college sports days. After about thirty minutes, they have to cut the conversation short, but this time they exchange phone numbers.

REBECCA'S STORY

Rebecca goes to Starbucks and sits by a man named Robert, who notices her beautiful blue eyes and has to say something. "Ma'am, I don't mean to be rude, but you have the most beautiful eyes I have ever seen." Rebecca blushes. They begin to exchange pleasantries and notice they have similar interests. Robert has been at his job for years and has been married for fifteen years. He seems very secure, confident, and observant. She can't believe how he's made her feel in such a short period of time. She begins to reminisce about those similar types of conversations she had when she first met her husband. After several years of marriage, things are slowly deteriorating. The passion, communication, and love seems to have left years ago. After about forty minutes of conversation, Rebecca needs to head back to work.

Robert and Rebecca go to the same Starbucks the next day with the hope of running into each other and continuing their conversation. As she walks into Starbucks, she notices Robert sitting in the back working on his computer. Rebecca asks to join him at his table. Before she can even sit down, Robert notices her hair and comments on how it brings out the color of her eyes. Wow, does he have her attention. It has been years since she has received that kind of attention.

Before they leave Starbucks, they exchange phone numbers and make plans to see each other.

MY POINT

Early in the marriage, we still date and flatter one another. We call each other pet names such as boo, honey bun, and baby. Spending time together is not optional but mandatory. Unfortunately, after a few years of marriage, this thing called life happens. We change jobs, have children, and do so many other things that disrupt the flow of the relationship.

I mentioned earlier that to deprive means to deny our spouse of something. So how do we deny our spouses? We refrain from giving them attention, recognition, compliments, time, and daily deposits. Babies cry for attention and adults die for attention. Each day I make a point to make deposits in my wife's love account. A deposit is saying or doing something that adds value to who and what she already is. Throughout the year, I send my wife flowers for no apparent reason. I get up in the morning and make her breakfast and lunch because I enjoy serving. I am so blessed that God allowed our paths to cross, and my goal is always to do something to demonstrate my gratitude. This behavior is part of the culture we have established in our home. We are a home where daily deposits of love are a way of life.

I got married so that I could always be dating and chasing my wife. Never stop dating.

STATE THE OBVIOUS

Infidelity is always a choice, so I don't want people to ever assume that it's their spouses that caused them to be unfaithful. Just like you choose what you eat, you also decide what you do, and you should never absolve yourself of personal responsibility. My intent is to create such a strong bond in your marriage that nothing on the outside has a chance of invading your marriage, not even flirtatious conversation.

How often do you notice something different about your spouse?

How often do you make love deposits?

Are you still dating your spouse or have you become complacent?

WHY IS THIS IMPORTANT?

When a man gets a flu shot, a nurse injects him with a small portion of the flu virus. The shot builds a stronger immune response to the virus so that when his body detects the virus, his immune system will recognize the virus and fight it on his behalf. His immune systems will tell the virus: There are a lot of bodies you can infect, but this is one that will not participate.

Deposits and recognition operate in a similar way to your immune system. When you make deposits into your spouse, it registers and strengthens your spouse's emotional bank account. When someone else attempts to make a deposit, it has little value because your spouse already has a full emotional bank account. Your spouse politely says thank you and keeps moving. Make it a point to intentionally uplift, compliment, and encourage your spouse. Your motivation should not be so that no one will approach your spouse, but it lets your spouse know you are paying attention.

RECOGNITION

In the two examples above, Harvey and Rebecca were enticed because they heard things that were foreign to their ears. It had been years since either had received any compliments, attention, or love deposits. Infidelity doesn't start with couples going to a hotel for sex; it begins when most couples deny their spouses some form of recognition. In no way does this excuse one or both parties for violating and disregarding their vows; it is only intended to bring to light the necessity for our investment in one another.

SOMEONE'S ON THE PREY

My wife and I went to the bank to make a transaction. As she was conducting business, I decided to wait in some chairs next to where HR Block was doing taxes. As she began to leave, I noticed a young man staring at my wife. Before he could approach her, she was already walking toward me. The young man recognized that, and his conscience seemingly condemned him. He approached me and said, "I'm sorry for staring at your wife, but I did not know she was taken." I said,

"If I'd seen her, I probably would have tried to talk to her as well. I put in a lot of work with my spouse, so it would have taken more than a conversation on your part." Looking puzzled, he walked off. I make deposits daily and in no way feel threatened by other men. I take their advances as a compliment.

ADDING VALUE

My intent each day is to increase the value my spouse feels through deposits, which strengthens her immunity from outside influences. It doesn't take a conscious effort to make a withdrawal, but it does take being intentional to make deposits. Anytime I make withdrawals and refrain from making deposits, I leave her with a negative balance.

Each time I conduct a marriage workshop and the topic of sex arrives, people get squeamish. It's something that most people desire but hesitate to discuss openly. Although sex is not the most important part of the marriage, it does play an intricate role. Studies vary when it comes to happiness and sex; however, most studies agree that lack of sex creates a decline in the relationship.

Can we be open and honest about sex?

Is there anything that's keeping your relationship from having more intimate sex?

What value do you place on deposits?

SELFISHNESS IN OPERATION

A woman took her husband to the doctor because he had severe chest pains. After examination, the doctor told her her husband was suffering from stress. The doctor asked if her husband could wait in the other room so he could give his wife some instructions.
"Your husband is ill, but he can have a full recovery if you do three things."
"What do you need me to do?" she asked.
"Do his chores, cook every day, and have sex with him three times a week."
When the wife went into the other room, her husband asked: "What did the doctor say?"
"You're getting ready to die."

THINGS THAT CAN AFFECT SEX IN THE MARRIAGE FOR WOMEN

Although my wife and I have agreed not to tell each other *no,* there are things I can do that can hurt our sexual relationship. A woman's mega need is security, so when I speak to her, I have to speak her security language. Anytime she believes her security is at risk, she can shut down. Sex is especially a sensitive matter if a woman has come out of a relationship where infidelity and trust were issues.

SCENARIO 1

It's football season, and the husband tells his wife he's headed to the sports bar to watch football and he's not sure what time he will be home. He says he's meeting some guys from work and some old college football teammates. He'll see her later. There is nothing wrong with this statement, but depending upon their relationship status, it can make his wife insecure. She may or may not know everyone there, and she might be skeptical about where he is going.

REVISED VERSION

"Honey, it's football season, and I'm getting ready to go to Johnny's Sports Bar to watch the Dallas Cowboys play the Giants. The game starts at 3 p.m., but I'll be back home by 6 p.m. By the way, if you happen to leave the house, stop by so I can make the guys jealous when they see I married a model. On second thought, let's just go together, if you have time."

Nothing is wrong in the first scenario, but it leaves room for the woman's insecurities. His wife wonders what time he'll be home and what his relationship is with the people he will be meeting. She wonders if other women will be there, and if so, why he didn't invite her. With the revised version, the husband gives much more detail. He is attempting to leave no doubt about what he is doing and where he is going. He is speaking her language of security and also meeting her second basic need, which is open and honest communication.

Men are not naturally geared to give details because it can make them feel they are not trusted; however, if they want their wives to feel secure, they must put forth an effort.

Remember guys, if she is insecure, it affects the type of *sex* we receive. That's usually enough motivation to get most men talking.

What are some things you noticed that could have been done better to cater to his wife's huge need of security?

Is it too much to ask for men to be a little more specific and sensitive?

How can giving more detail increase intimacy?

Even if the husband and wife have a good trusting relationship, should the husband still cater toward her mega need for security? Why or why not?

THINGS THAT CAN AFFECT SEX IN THE MARRIAGE FOR MEN

SCENARIO 2

A woman gets mad at her husband because he didn't clean out the garage as promised. She is sitting in the living room with the children, and the moment his feet hit the carpet, she says, "You claimed you were going to clean the garage out so that I could park my car inside! My safety is important to me because I hate getting in my car in the morning in the dark. Every time you say you are going to do something, you never keep your word! What are you teaching your children?"

A man's mega need is respect, and when disrespected, it cuts him to the core. Disrespect is the quickest way a woman can isolate her husband, pushing him into emotional abandonment and sexual withdrawal.

REVISED VERSION

As soon as he gets home, his wife says, "Hello, honey, how was your day at work? After you get settled, can I take you to the restaurant in our neighborhood? I need some advice on something."

Once they arrive at the restaurant, she says, "I love you, and I'm grateful because you are a great provider. I wanted to speak with you because when you tell me you are going to do something, I trust you. When that doesn't happen, it can create trust issues in our relationship. You said you were going to clean out the garage so I could park my car. I hate going outside in the morning and getting in my car in the dark. Is there something you need from me to help you do this?

SUMMARY

In the first scenario, his wife was upset, and I'm not saying she shouldn't have been. However, she berated the husband in front of the children as soon as he walked in the door and told him he was setting a bad example for the kids. She disrespected him, and the result could be isolation.

What did you notice about the woman's behavior in the first scenario?

How could she have approached the situation from a healthier perspective?

What is meant by Every action requires an equal or opposite reaction, and how does this apply to this situation?

How did she violate his need for respect?

SECOND SCENARIO

In the second scenario, the wife greeted her husband at the door. She asked if they could leave the home because she had something she wanted to ask. This way the kids would not see a blowup if it happened. She started the conversation off by stating he was a good provider before she mentioned her concern. She was speaking his language of respect.

When we don't speak each other's language, the other party is not listening.

Is it safe to assume the conversation ended on a much healthier note? List some things she did differently in the second scenario.

If we desire a great sex life, we must be intentional about our approach in every area of our marriages. Our approaches will affect our desired outcomes. Although sex is more about emotions for women than for men, everything we do and say affects the type of sex we receive. We must become acquainted with our partners' basic needs as well as their love languages. If we are not speaking to their basic needs, nor their love languages, it could make for some lonely nights in the bedroom. Once we learn to serve our spouses in these areas, we will begin to experience sex on a new level.

Takeaways

- Talk openly and honestly about sex before and during the marriage.
- Make daily deposits.
- Never use sex as a weapon.
- Agree to never deprive each other sexually.
- This is a lifelong commitment, so sometimes it takes being creative.

Notes

[1] https://www.truthaboutdeception.com/cheating-and-infidelity/stats-about-infidelity.html

[2] [CC BY-SA 4.0 (http://creativecommons.org/licenses/by-sa/4.0)], via Wikimedia Commons

CHAPTER 7

Love Is a Verb
Walk the Talk

Actions speak much louder than words. If you think about it, they are your words, because your actions are what people are reading.

The Savior demonstrated his love by three means: serving, suffering, and sacrifice. "A new commandment I give unto you, that ye love one another; as I have loved you, that ye also love one another. By this shall all men know that ye are my disciples if ye have love one to another" (John 13:34–35). If we say we are his disciples, serving, suffering, and sacrificing should be shown in our *actions.* Love is a verb.

> *The above Scripture is probably one of the most profound verses in the Bible. A new commandment—this indicates the*

> *first commandment needed to be abolished. God gave the people of Israel 613 laws, which they broke continually. Each time they broke the law, they had to offer up a sacrifice for their sin. Since no one could keep the law, God replaced it with something much greater: love.*

"For all the law is fulfilled in one word, *even* in this; thou shalt love thy neighbor as thyself" (Galatians 5:14). How is it possible for one word to fulfill the whole law, and why would God use this one word? God was stating that love was the summation of the entire law, and if I understand the law of love, the rest of the 613 laws fall in line with it.

> If I love my brother, I will not attempt to sleep with his wife.
> If I love my brother, I will not attempt to kill him or do him any harm. If I love my brother, I will not speak any evil of him.
> Love conquers all.

Early Childhood

As a child, I had the pleasure of being raised in a dual parent household. Although this was quite the norm in those days, we can all agree that times have changed. It is common today to see children in a single parent household, and the other parent is not actively involved in their lives. During an interview, I was asked about the root of some of the issues I see in our society. It begins with the destruction and breakdown of the family unit. When the family unit erodes, it affects children in almost every aspect of our society—from education, social skills, emotions, and self-esteem to our prison population. The presence of the father is especially critical for the emotional success of our children. Children can do well in single parent households, but the chance of achievement increases with the presence of an involved father.

- 63% of youth suicides are from fatherless homes (US Dept. Of Health/Census) – 5 times the average.
- 90% of all homeless and runaway children are from fatherless homes – 32 times the average.
- 85% of all children who show behavior disorders come from fatherless homes – 20 times the average (Centers for Disease Control and Prevention)
- 80% of rapists with anger problems come from fatherless homes –14 times the average (Justice & Behavior, Vol 14, p. 403–26)
- 71% of all high school dropouts come from fatherless homes – 9 times the average (National Principals Association Report)

~ The Fatherless Generation[1]

This is why having healthy relationships is critical, because what we do affects more than just us. Our children and the next generation are depending upon you and me.

Both of my parents were excellent providers. My father worked hard each day at a local milk company, and my mother was a homemaker and cosmetologist. My dad didn't make a lot of money, but our family never suffered financially, nor can I ever recall a time I went without the necessities. Each day I came home from school, there was a meal sitting on the stove, and our house was always clean.

Emotional Agreement

Several years before I met my spouse, I went out on a date with a seemingly promising young lady. She was attractive, no kids, good job, educated, and owned her home. From the outside, everything looked appealing. During our first date, she spoke very passionately about her divorce. She gave explicit details of her ex's extramarital affairs, verbal abuse, and selfish mentality. I empathized with her as I listened to the hurt and frustration in her voice. I'm not sure why, but something in me told me to ask her how long she had been divorced. She said ten years! *Wow.* She was speaking as if it were yesterday. She had allowed her past to affect her future by becoming a victim instead of a victor. Needless to say, I never called her again. Our experiences will make us bitter or better, but we get to choose.

> *Our past causes us to be victims or victors.*

Life finds us in three stages:

> Going through,
> coming out, or
> getting ready to go through something.

Everyone has something in his or her past or present that's emotionally challenging. Before marriage, there is a propensity to overlook a person's emotional issues and assume they will dissipate over time, which is an unhealthy perspective and not one I recommend. We must enter the relationship based upon what *is* and not leave our future up to a desired expectation. This perspective often leads to disappointment, and disappointment can lead to bitterness. Do you accept your spouse for who he or she is?

> *"Disappointment is the gap between expectation and reality." ~ John Maxwell*

When I met my wife, she had just ended a marriage of twenty years. Apart from a few relationships, her ex-husband was the only man she had been with. From time to time I would ask her—my then girlfriend and now wife—how she was doing since the divorce. She would always tell me she was okay. However, in my spirit I didn't feel as if everything was okay. How could someone be married for that length of time and not feel the residual effects of divorce? She was in denial and had learned to suppress her emotions.

One day I called her and asked her to do me a favor. She said okay. I asked her to visit her ex-husband and just talk. She said she wouldn't. I can't say what I said was wise, but I gave her an ultimatum. I told her that if she didn't go and visit with him, we could no longer date. Not knowing why, she reluctantly agreed. She called him and set an appointment for the following day.

They both agreed to meet at his apartment. Kim's ex-husband assumed that she was attempting to rekindle their twenty-year marriage and that I was trying to get rid of her, but this was not the case. When they divorced, it was rather abrupt, and neither had closure. I knew she could not open a new door until she closed the one she had just come through.

Are there any doors you have come through that are not closed?

If so, how has this affected your relationships?

What have you learned from your past experiences that can be of value to a future relationship?

When you talk about your ex, are you disparaging or do you talk about it from a perspective of growth? [Note: if you don't talk about it from a position of growth, you are not ready to move forward.]

TAKING A CHANCE

Before her visit, I began to prepare myself emotionally for the possibility of being disappointed. After long-term breakups, there is sometimes the proclivity to attempt to rekindle that old flame. Although we know there's a strong possibility the relationship will not succeed, the *known* can have a much stronger pull on the heart than the new and unknown. We know what we can expect from our exes, but we are not sure what to expect from this new relationship, so we sometimes try one more time to read the same book, even if we know the ending is going to be the same.

THE CHALLENGE

I know what you might be thinking—what if she had decided she wanted to get back with him? What if she realized she still loved him? After all, this was her children's father and the man she had shared most of her adult life with. The harsh but simple reality is when people leave you, they weren't yours to have. I'm a firm believer that what God has for you is for you alone, and you don't have to share them emotionally or physically with someone else. If she had told me she wanted to go back to him, I would have wished them the best and thanked her for the experience. Sometimes if we love people, we have to be willing to set them free. This does not mean that I am impervious to hurt or disappointment, because I would have been devastated. However, these are things that are best to know before, rather than after, you say *I do.*

HER DECISION

After their meeting, she called me crying. I assumed that her ex-husband had done something to harm her because she had come out of an abusive situation, but no, that wasn't it. She was crying happy tears because she understood why I wanted her to speak with her ex, and knew I'd asked her to because I loved her. She had called some of her friends and told them I wanted her to meet with her ex, and they had assured her this was my way of bringing the relationship to an end. However, upon leaving his apartment, she realized that she had not had closure and had needed answers to many questions. They both had the opportunity to apologize for their shortcomings during the marriage with transparency, and agreed to move forward amicably. I then asked her if she wanted to get back together with him. She emphatically said *no.* At this point, I knew the healing process could begin and she was emotionally ready to move forward. If your partner has no closure from a previous relationship, you're only getting half of him or her. Closure provides you with the whole person.

Is there something in your life that stirs up your emotions but has not been brought to the surface?

What was your childhood like?

What type of example were your parents? Children tend to marry people just like their parents....

Before we got married, we agreed to not hold our past, or anything emotionally challenging, against the other person. Instead, we have chosen to support and love each other through our past and current circumstances. We need to heal our past before entering a new relationship with new challenges. Can you accept those conditions?

The Missing Piece

When a man is walking in the forest, all he sees are the trees around him; however, were he to look at the forest from an elevated position, he would appreciate the entire forest. It wasn't until I left home for the military that I had a genuine appreciation for my parents, as well as a clear understanding of our dysfunctional patterns. As a child, I expected my parents to fulfill their duties by being responsible providers, but they were often ignorant of my emotional needs. (When I use the word ignorant, I mean lacking knowledge.) If these emotional needs go unaddressed, it can cause children to live a life with low self-esteem, insecurity, lack of confidence, and a list of other issues.

Our Dysfunction

Dysfunction actually means to malfunction—something doesn't work the way it should. Unfortunately, to dysfunctional families, dysfunction looks normal.

I can remember watching television shows that showed parents hugging their children, and wondering what it felt like to be embraced. Unfortunately, the closest I came to hugging my parents was when I was disciplined. As I mentioned earlier, this lack of validation left me on a life-long journey of seeking acceptance, which was sometimes sought in unhealthy places. When children are validated and accepted at home, it's harder for others outside the home to influence them negatively.

As I previously discussed, love is a verb and verbs demonstrate action. That action has to be in line with our words. For love to come full circle, word and deed have to agree. When these two are combined, they have a positive effect on the emotional and physical well-being of our spouses and our children. Word and deed are Siamese twins that can never be separated. We can tell our loved ones we love them, but our actions will always be their confirmation. I can't hear what you are saying when your actions overshadow your words. "But be ye doers of the word, and not hearers only, deceiving your own selves" (James 1:22).

Give at least two examples of your love that demonstrated word and deed.

Why are words and deeds important when it comes to love?

What are you willing to give up to go up? I love to work out, and others often ask me how I got so buff and what they can do to improve their physique. I realized years ago that it's not about what you want but what you are willing to sacrifice to get it that counts.

It is easy to do the things that are convenient, but with love comes sacrifice. If we only do things that are convenient and there is no sacrifice, our love is not real—it's superficial.

We have all heard stories of women forgoing their careers to support their husband's dreams, or of parents moving to another state to put their children in the best schools. My wife took on the role of sole provider so I could finish my college degree and focus on studying. She understood that love required a sacrifice, and without sacrifice, love had no chance of being sustained.

What have you given up to demonstrate your love?

What are you willing to give up to demonstrate your love?

What effect do you believe this sacrifice can have on the marriage?

Why is it easier to say the words than to demonstrate love?

Whether we know it or not, we are influencing others through our behavior. We should ask ourselves how we are influencing others with our marriages, especially our kids. Children will operate according to what they have seen and experienced. People hear what we say but are influenced by our actions.

"Leadership is influence—nothing more, nothing less." ~ John Maxwell

When children see parents disagree, they get to witness our character in operation. They can see arrogance, pride, and selfishness or humility, meekness, and a heart filled with grace.

My Greatest Life Lesson

My mother never spoke respectfully to my father. My dad would ask her a question, and she would respond in a very disparaging tone. Until the day my father passed, he never said one word in retaliation. For some reason, he always let my mother have the last word. This made my dad appear weak, and in my eyes, less of a man. After all, this was at a time when most men were the sole providers and leaders of the household. What kind of man was my father to never defend his position, or to at least have the last word?

One day, while home on leave from the military, my father and I were conversing on the front porch. For some strange reason, he asked me if I wanted to know why he never said anything back to my mother. I gladly said yes. This is what I had been waiting to hear for years. I was not prepared for his answer. He said, "Someone in the house has to operate like they have some sense."

Do you have to have the last word?

That statement readjusted my values and caused a paradigm shift. My dad was about five foot ten, but he immediately became much bigger in my sight. I no longer believe I have to have the last word or be right. My father was not weak but strong and filled with wisdom, beyond anything I could comprehend. He never wanted us to see him acting in an unloving manner toward my mom, so he suffered in silence. His actions remind me of one of my favorite Scriptures: "He was oppressed, and he was afflicted, yet he opened not his mouth: he is brought as a lamb to the slaughter, and as a sheep before her shearers is dumb, so he openeth not his mouth" (Isaiah 53:7).

> *Silence is often misinterpreted but never misquoted. ~ Unknown*

Love is a verb and verbs show action; love can't just exist in speech, it also must exist in deed. If it exists in word and not in deed, we have half the story. When it comes to marriage, everything we do and say matters. It imperative that we tell our spouses we love them, but it is more important that we demonstrate that love. Sometimes my wife might be cleaning up, and I'll ask her to stop and sit on my lap. I look into her eyes and tell her how much I love and appreciate her marrying me and being an excellent spouse. Most mornings I wake up early to fix her breakfast and ensure she has a lunch for work. I could easily sleep for an extra hour in the morning, but those sacrifices of my time are worth the investment, because they generate a great return.

Again, if our marriages are to succeed, love has to be a verb. Our spouses can't just hear those words; our actions should always be their confirmation. If not, we will be talking loudly with no one listening.

Why is it important to say I love you and demonstrate that love?

What are some ways this can be demonstrated with your spouse?

Love without Conditions

One of the most powerful ways of demonstrating love is loving our spouses without conditions. If love comes with conditions, it's a clear indication that love didn't exist from the beginning. This means the relationship was based on convenience, lust, or both. If my spouse gains weight, loses weight, loses her job, or whatever situation might occur, it will not interfere with my love. Remember, a woman's primary need is security, and from the moment she senses that love is conditional, she can become withdrawn.

Love is patient,
love is kind.
It does not envy,
it does not boast,
it is not proud.

It does not dishonor others,

it is not self-seeking,
it is not easily angered,
it keeps no record of wrongs.
Love does not delight in evil
but rejoices with the truth.

It always protects,
always trusts,
always hopes,
always perseveres.

~ 1 Corinthians 13:4–7 NIV

The part I love about this verse is *love keeps no record of wrongs.* What would this demonstration of love do for our marriages? It would grow us, and the byproduct is that it would build our marriages.

Takeaways

- Get counseling for your emotional brokenness before going into a marriage. Apologize, forgive, and heal from past hurt.
- Love is one of the most frequently used words in our society. *I love you* easily rolls off the tongue with seamless effort. However, if I say I love my spouse, it is going to have to be demonstrated by my actions, so it is imperative that I love in word but also in demonstration. One without the other will leave our spouse, children, and those we love unfulfilled.
- Love is a verb, and verbs show action.
- Love is 1 Corinthians 13:4–7.

Notes

[1] https://thefatherlessgeneration.wordpress.com/statistics/

CHAPTER 8

Be Right or Be Fruitful

Being right is not always fruitful, but being fruitful is always right.

Very seldom do both parties agree that their marriage needs some intervention by a third party. Usually, one party is interested in counseling and has to coerce the other party into going.

Counseling can be very beneficial for marriage when couples go for the right reasons and both see the need for intervention.

ROBERT AND JENNY

Robert and Jenny went to counseling because Jenny didn't feel valued in the relationship. Within the last several months, Robert had become verbally abusive, worked late hours, and spent very little time at home with her and the kids.

Despite her many pleas to Robert, her concerns went unheard. Finally, she asked Robert if he would be willing to go and speak with a third party regarding their marriage. Although reluctant, Robert agreed to counseling. After the second counseling session, the counselor informed Robert that he was self-centered and some adjustments needed to be made if he wanted to save his marriage. Before the counselor could finish getting the words out of his mouth, Jenny replied: "See? The counselor agrees with me. I told you so." As they were leaving his office, neither one of them spoke a word to each other on the way home and slept in separate beds that night.

REVIEW

If the counselor pointed out the discrepancy, should not this have resolved their issue?

Why were they still at odds with each other after counseling?

Why did they go to counseling in the first place?

Did Robert go because the relationship needed intervention, or did he go to appease his wife?

FYI—How to Get a Spouse to Agree to Counseling

Counselors often express what is already apparent, but the advice is sometimes better received from a third party.

Usually, one party favors counseling and the other party only goes to appease to the other person. It makes a huge difference when both sides agree. So how do we get our significant others to willingly agree to counsel? One of my favorite leadership sayings is that people support what people help create.

A typical conversation might look like this: Jenny approaches Robert and says, "We have not been of one accord for the last several months, and I think we should seek counsel about our issues." Nothing is necessarily wrong with this approach, except it is her idea instead of his.

What if she said the same thing but made it his idea?

> Robert, we have been having issues for the last several months.
> What do you suggest we do to get back to being of one accord?
> Do you think we need counseling, and if so, who do you have in mind?
> If we go, what do you hope we will accomplish?
> How early would you like to start our sessions?

The goal is to make counseling the other person's idea and not yours. If it is your spouse's idea, you will not have to coerce or bribe him or her into going. Remember, people support what people help create, and no one wants to see his idea or suggestion *fail.* Try it; it works.

BACK TO THE ACTION

So what happened with Robert and Jenny, and why was there no reconciliation at the end of the counseling session? What occurred in this situation is prevalent during disagreements, and even in counseling sessions. I know very few couples whose counseling has helped their marriage when only one of them wants it. Why? If couples are going to attend counseling, they need be in agreement as to why they are going and what they hope to obtain from attending.

REALITY CHECK

If you recall, the counselor told Robert he was self-centered and if he wanted to save his marriage he would need to make some adjustments. Jenny jumped on those words with: "The counselor agrees with me. I told you so." Jenny's intent for going to counseling wasn't about reconciliation but about being right and winning. If your goal is about winning, that means the other person loses. What man wants to feel as if he is a loser, and who wants to hear *I told you so*? That's why, at the end of the session, there was no reconciliation—because of the intent and the approach.

The question we all have to answer is, do you want to win and be right or do you want to reconcile your differences? Your answer will determine your approach, and your approach will determine your outcome. As for me and my house, we have determined that being fruitful is far better than being right.

What do you hope to get out of a disagreement?

What is the best approach to resolve disagreements?

If intervention is needed, what should the approach be of both parties?

Does who is right take precedence over what's right?

PAUL AND JEN

It was a Friday night, and Paul was headed to the local sports bar to hang out with some old college buddies. Paul had a good job as a program manager for a major software company, and he was excited about sharing his success with his old friends. Jen was a stay-at-home mom and a volunteer on the school board. They had been married for nine years and had two children.

Paul's college buddies were in town for the weekend, and it had been several years since they had seen each other. However, before he could get out the door, he was confronted by his wife, Jen.

In a firm tone, Jen said, "You always leave me at home with the children, and we never go anywhere as a couple, and you come back wanting sex. A real man would never neglect his wife."

Paul, in a defensive manner said, "What do you mean, I always ignore you? Last week I took you to Texas Roadhouse for a quiet dinner. You are always on my back about something, and you don't appreciate how hard I work for this family. Do you know how many women would love to be in your position?"

Jen kept insisting that Paul was wrong and Paul kept insisting that Jen was wrong. They began conversing at 9 p.m. and ended at around 2 a.m. When the conversation concluded, there was still no sense of resolution, just frustration.

REVIEW

What did Jen say that caused greater tension, and could she have addressed this differently?

What did Paul say that caused greater tension and could he have addressed the situation differently?

What should be our goal during a disagreement?

Many of us can relate to having arguments that last well into the night and end without clarity. Couples often forget the origin of the conflict, because many other issues surface. Instead of one item needing addressing, there are now several open conversations. Things from the past, present, and sometimes things that have not even transpired are part of the discussion. Just remember, anytime a disagreement is everywhere, the discussion is going nowhere.

When we approach agreements with the right intent, it will change the outcome.

Disagreements should never be about being right, but approached with the intent of reconciliation.

Being right is about you; being reconciled is about *us.* As I've said, most counseling is ineffective because couples enter the session with the intent of proving the other wrong rather than seeking reconciliation. A marriage succeeds when *the health of the marriage* influences our decisions, which is greater than the wants and needs of the individuals.

Most business decisions are approached with a win-win mindset, and this is the same course needed for success in your relationship. If you win and I win, the relationship wins. Nobody gets everything, but we all get some of what we want. It's called compromise.

JEN'S PERSPECTIVE

As she approached her husband, she said, "You *always* leave me at home, and we *never* go anywhere as a couple." It's rather obvious that Jen didn't feel valued and might have felt this way for quite some time. Her response is what happens when concerns build up over time and never get addressed.

The words *always* and *never* are absolutes and should not be mentioned during the conversation. Nothing is always, and nothing is never. These words add fuel to the fire and place the other person in defense and attack mode.

"If you were a real man, you would never neglect me." A man's number one need is respect. The fastest way to get a man to shut down and go into his cave is when he believes his manhood has been challenged or feels he has been emasculated. We must address and attack the issue, but never attack the person.

Based upon Jen's tone, sex might be used as a weapon later on because she felt neglected. When not approached with the right tools, it compounds our issues.

PAUL'S PERSPECTIVE

Paul went on the defensive because of the way Jen approached him. He chose an opposite reaction rather than an equal one and began to think about the sacrifices he'd made for his family. Apparently his efforts were not appreciated. He did not help his cause by saying, "You know how many women would love to be in your shoes?"—correctly interpreted as *shut up and be happy. I'm a good provider.* Paul appeared to have a sense of entitlement because he was the breadwinner, and if he desired, he could have another woman on the side.

What's your perspective about Paul's response?

WHAT WE CAN LEARN

Whenever something needs to be discussed, our approach will determine the outcome. From their perspectives, Jen and Paul had correct perspectives. However, just because we believe something doesn't make it true. I'm always reminded of my dad's choice: "A soft answer turneth away wrath: but grievous words stir up anger" (Proverbs 15:1). We never want to approach conversations from an attacking standpoint but with a heart desiring resolution. Anytime our conversation begins with *you always* or *you never,* the night will be long and usually sleepless.

HOW COULD JEN CHANGE HER APPROACH?

Let's replay this scenario and look at another option. Paul tells Jen he is heading to the local sports bar to hang out with some old college buddies. Jen feels left out, but she kisses him and asks what time he will be home. Paul says 11 p.m.

When Paul returns, Jen is waiting for him as he comes through the door. She kisses him and asks him if he had fun, which he did. She asks if he'd like to watch a movie with her because it's a Friday night, which he agrees to. Before the film starts, she tells him she's really glad he had a good time and she appreciates how he provides for the family. And then she becomes vulnerable with her pain. She tells him that sometimes she feels insecure and neglected, and asks him if he thinks they can spend more time together as a couple in future.

What is different about this approach?

Do you believe this approach would produce a different result?

What happens when we use absolutes such as you always or you never?

What should our goal be during those difficult conversations?

Did she address Paul's need for respect?

Give an example of another approach she could have used.

WHAT COULD PAUL HAVE DONE DIFFERENTLY?

Sometimes it's not about what's stated, but about what's not being said. Listen carefully. When Jen said, "You always leave me home and never take me anywhere," Jen already knew Paul spent time with her, but she desired a little more quality time. Because Paul was disconnected and consumed with his selfish intentions, he heard Jen, but he wasn't listening.

What if Paul had said he was sorry for not spending as much time with Jen and the kids as he'd like? Paul would have acknowledged her feelings and taken responsibility for his neglect, which would have eased or removed the tension in the conversation. One of the greatest stress releasers during a discussion is when we are accountable for our actions before we justify them. He could have asked their neighbors or his sister to keep the kids for a few hours, and they could have both gone to meet his college buddies together. He would have then validated her and removed any reason for her to feel insecure. When we learn to operate from our hearts and not our heads, we can get this type of response.

FOOD FOR THOUGHT

Our responses can generate a win-win in most situations.

If the roles were reversed and this happened to us, what type of treatment would I desire?

What is different about the approach Paul could have taken?

Do you believe this approach would produce a different result?

What should our goal be during those difficult conversations?

Did Paul address her basic need for security? If yes, how?

Our children, family, friends, and neighbors watch how we interact with our spouses. We are teaching them what to do or what not to do through our actions. For those who claim Christianity, your relationship with your partner witnesses more to your faith than where you worship. If you want to influence your friends, let them see a healthy relationship between you and your spouse.

For My Spiritual Leaders—A Teaching Moment

If you serve in the ministry, your family should be your first ministry and not the church. Too often, religious leaders use their calling to the ministry as a license to neglect their families. I know many pastors who smile in public with their spouses but live a contentious and isolated life at home. This is generally because most of their time is spent investing in the ministry and very little time is invested in the marriage.

Leading begins at home before it begins anywhere else. "For if a man know not how to rule his own house, how shall he take care of the church of God?" (1 Timothy 3:5). If we can't lead in our homes, we will be challenged trying to lead and influence our congregants. However, when we learn to lead our families, leading the church is easy. The law of priorities places things in this order:

1. My relationship with God
2. My relationship with my spouse
3. My relationship with my children
4. My service to the church

When not positioned in this order, every Sunday we will have to pretend our families and we are content, and that's stressful.

Takeaways

- Being right is not always fruitful, but being fruitful is always right. Being right will not always generate growth; if our approach is to be fruitful, our disagreements should end with us growing. The word "fruitful" means to produce an increase. Our differences should provide an increase and draw us closer together. This is only possible when we change our perspectives and our approaches. When everyone grows, the marriage wins.

CHAPTER 9

Seek First to Understand

Until people are heard and understood, they will not listen to you.

Every day in many marriages around the world, something stated is taken completely out of context, creating frustration for both parties. Not knowing how to listen is one of the biggest issues couples face regarding communication. School teaches us how to speak, but very few schools teach us how to listen. "Wherefore, my beloved brethren, let every man be swift to hear, slow to speak, slow to wrath" (James 1:19). However, the problem is not in knowing this verse but in how we apply it.

TERRY AND DONNA

Terry and Donna met in college through some mutual friends. They both had an instant attraction to one another and began dating. Upon graduation, they married and hastily had three children. Both came from dysfunctional backgrounds and never saw a healthy marriage modeled. Their marriage experienced a significant amount of turbulence during the early years and complacency in the later ones. Despite their dysfunction, they had a date night every Saturday: something they implemented early on. Terry was not a big fan of date night, but he participated to keep the peace.

While coming back from a movie, Donna informed Terry that he made a lot of decisions for the house without her input, and she would like to discuss some of those decisions. Terry responded, "So you don't think or trust that I make the right decisions for this family? My father made most of the decisions in our home, and my mother appreciated his efforts. So what are you saying? I'm not a good husband?"

Donna shook her head in utter disbelief that he could jump to that conclusion so quickly when it was not what she was saying at all. A simple concern on Donna's part had turned into another sleepless night.

REVIEW

How could Terry have responded more empathetically?

Where did Terry get his leadership style from, and was it wrong?

Why did Donna feel the way she did?

Do you see anything wrong with her approach?

By no means am I attempting to indict anyone, because this is challenging for all of us. If we never witnessed a healthy resolution when interactions like these happened with our parents, how can we know the proper response?

All mechanics have some tools that aren't used very often. These tools cost thousands of dollars, and a technician may use them once a year. To most people, this might not make any sense, but these tools can save the mechanic hours on the job; when it's time to use one of these tools, it proves to have much value. In the same way, communication success depends on having the right tools and knowing when to use them.

HOW IS THIS APPLICABLE TO MARRIAGE?

We all have tools we use in our marriage, but we might not have the correct tools. A screwdriver can be used as a knife, but that's not its intended purpose. This is what we refer to as a form of perversion. When we read books and attend workshops, they are designed to equip us with the proper tools—tools which can help save time, effort, frustration, and even our marriages. When we place the right tools in our toolboxes, we can expect to experience great marriages.

MY FAVORITE TOOL

If we are willing, we can all change our listening behaviors, because becoming a better listener can be learned. Seeking to understand first and then to be understood places us on the correct path to becoming a skillful listener. Something amazing happens when we put someone else's concerns above ours. Even with tension in the air, we have just made the other person feel valued, appreciated, and listened to. Why is learning to listen so crucial for communication in marriage? People will not hear us until they realize they have been heard.

My favorite communication tool is ECIR, which is RICE spelled backward.

E - EMPATHIZE

C - CLARIFY

I - ISOLATE

R - RESPOND

ECIR IN ACTION

Each step is essential for successful communication. When my wife approaches me with one of my discrepancies, the first thing I do is:

> (E) EMPATHIZE – "I understand how you could feel that way, and if the roles were reversed, I'd feel the same way." Or I'd apologize if I was in the wrong.

My initial reaction is to empathize or apologize, depending upon the situation. Acknowledgment, acceptance, and being accountable is crucial to furthering the conversation.

(C) CLARIFY why she is upset to make sure I understand her concern. – "Let me make sure I fully understand your concern: you are upset because of __________." Clarification helps to eliminate misunderstanding. Too often we respond without understanding what has been stated. Remember, what's said and how it is interpreted are two different things.

(I) ISOLATE the concern to ensure this is the only reason she is upset. –"Is this the only thing that has you upset?" Isolation ensures no other issues are pending. Sometimes other issues need addressing, and this is a way of exposing these matters. Therefore, isolation ensures that the matter on the table is the only issue on the table. [Note: discuss and resolve one issue at a time.]

(R) RESPOND – Then I give her my response. After we have followed this process, then we respond. ECIR allows us to process what's being said before responding. Because of tension during disagreements, it's easy to respond without processing. This reaction creates further anxiety and extends the argument.

Not following this formula is the reason most disputes last into the night. However, once we believe we have been heard, we feel valued. Although we are disagreeing, a sense of love is still in the room. After the dispute has concluded, couples can cuddle without any reservations.

Terry and Donna had a big misunderstanding that could have easily been resolved. Unfortunately, none of the above steps were implemented. Donna expressed her heart but probably felt as if she should have kept her comments to herself. Terry was operating based on what he had seen growing up, and never had even considered how his decisions affected his wife.

If he'd followed the ECIR process, he would have heard what she was saying and seen the hurt in her heart. The ECIR process allows us to do something completely against our nature: listen. Donna just wanted to be part of the team and not feel like a spectator. Since Terry was not listening, Donna might end up choosing to shut down. When we shut down, it creates isolation, which is the quickest way toward separation or divorce. Before something is destroyed, it isolates itself first.

Practice ECIR next time you have a necessary discussion, and write the results here.

E

C

I

R

Takeways

- People will not listen to you until they know they have been heard.
- Seek to understand before being understood. Put yourself in the other person's shoes.

CHAPTER 10

Respect

Peace is not the absence of conflict, it is the ability to handle conflict by peaceful means. ~ Ronald Reagan

The longer I'm married, the better I've learned to handle disagreements. This doesn't indicate I have all the answers. We are still a work in progress. We have a very successful relationship, but even ours does not exist without challenges.

If a relationship exists without conflict, couples have learned to coexist together. When handled properly, conflicts can be healthy for the relationship. If handled irresponsibly, they can destroy the relationship and leave lasting scars.

Conflicts are inevitable, but we will handle them with respect for one another.

When I was six, my first grade teacher emphasized the old saying that sticks and stones may break my bones, but words will never hurt me. This might sound adorable, but it's far from the truth. Sometimes words do more damage than physical abuse.

Let's iterate a few tips to help manage healthy conflict:

- Disagreements should always be about understanding one another and reconciliation. My intent should not be to prove you wrong but to understand.
- Conflicts are resolved faster when what's right supersedes who's right.
- When speaking to one another, speak to each other's basic need: A man's biggest need is respect and a woman's biggest need is security.

What example will our actions be before our God, our children, and others? With disagreements come emotions. Depending upon what you have experienced, it is easier to respond from an emotional state than a rational perspective. Just remember we have to live with the consequences of our choices.

Sometimes we don't get what we want; we get what we allow. If someone disrespects me and it goes unaddressed, I have just communicated that disrespect is acceptable. From the very beginning, our must-haves should be on display, and we should never be willing to compromise our values for the sake of saying we're in a relationship. If we compromise our values, shame on us and not them.

I remember vividly a conversation I had with my wife when we were dating. It was about 8:30 p.m. on a Tuesday night, and we were conversing before we went to bed. During this time, Kim lived in Killeen, Texas, and I lived in Austin, Texas, which is about fifty-five miles from where she was. Kim was coming out of a twenty-year marriage and was very emotional. I expressed to her over the phone that I believed she was using me to rebound. No sooner did those words come out of my mouth when she began to tear into me. She said, "You think I come to see you every weekend because I'm just using you?" She then expressed some words I will not repeat. After she finished her tirade, I politely hung up the phone. I wasn't willing to be spoken to like that.

Do you walk away from power displays, especially during the initial dating stages, if you're being disrespected or mistreated?

What is it about you that makes you willing to accept less?

If you know your worth, you won't settle for less. Why settle for less when you are worth more? You'll never expect more if you think you are less than. Do you know your worth?

How is your self-image, and how do you see yourself?

People treat me based upon what I allow. What does that mean to you?

Within a few minutes Kim called me back and asked, "Why did you hang up on me?" I asked Kim, "Do you like me?" and she said yes. I said, "Don't ever talk to me in that manner, and if you believe that it's necessary, don't call or speak to me again." This response surprised her a lot, because she was accustomed to debating and arguing with her ex-husband. I didn't raise my voice or use unacceptable language, but I did allow my must-haves to take center stage. I knew if this went unaddressed, I would see that behavior again.

If addressed at a later date, your words have less power; however, when corrected immediately, you set a clear standard. To this day, we have never had to have that type of conversation again.

I mentioned earlier it's a good idea to keep our basic needs in mind while communicating. The quickest way to get your partner to go into his or her cave is to violate one of these needs.

WOMEN'S BASIC NEEDS

1. Security
2. Open and honest communication
3. Affection
4. Leadership

MEN'S BASIC NEEDS

1. Respect and honor
2. Sex
3. Friendship
4. Support

SUE AND JOE

Sue and Joe had been married for several years, but much of that time was spent separated. During their separation, Joe fathered a child. It was not long before Sue received word about the other child and was devastated. Both of them had children, but none together.

One day Joe and Sue saw each other at a party and began to chat. Sue was having a hard time financially, and Joe was suffering from loneliness. The idea of getting back together began to surface; after all, they were still married. Two weeks after meeting at the party, they were back together under the same roof.

One day Joe's child's mother called and said the child was sick and she needed his assistance. Joe mentioned the phone call to Sue, and within minutes he was out the door.

Upon his return, Sue had some harsh words regarding his departure. "You are a no-good man just like your father! I have no idea why I thought to give you the time of day! I know you and your baby's momma were having sex, and nothing is wrong with that bastard child of yours."

Joe looked exasperated. "What in the hell are you talking about? My kid is sick, and you think I'm out trying to have sex? Now I understand why I left you in the first place!"

SUE

What basic need did Sue violate, and how did she violate it?

Was she premature in getting back together with Joe?

What was Sue's motive for wanting to be with Joe?

Could Sue's comments cause irreparable damage to the relationship? If so, how?

How could Sue have spoken to Joe's basic need?

JOE

What basic need did Joe violate and how?

Was Joe premature in getting back with Sue?

What was Joe's motivation for getting back together?

Could Joe's comments cause irreparable damage to the relationship? If so, how?

How could Joe have spoken to her basic need?

Is it true that when you start off wrong, you end up wrong? The relationship was doomed before they moved under the same roof. Both parties had ulterior motives for reuniting that had nothing to do with saving their marriage. As I said in an earlier chapter, one of the reasons mergers fail is because of flawed intentions. Love was not the driving force; their selfish ambitions were. The eruption by both parties had little to do with the circumstances and more to do with their initial motive. We reap what we sow.

"For a war to be, just three conditions are necessary - public authority, just cause and the right motive." ~ Ernest Hemingway

THE BYPRODUCT–DAMAGE

Although Sue knew the conditions of the relationship, she didn't accept the child nor the circumstances attached. When Joe had to go and see about the child, it created concerns on Sue's part—*distrust.* The child was a constant reminder of something she and Joe had never had, and of the intimate relationship he had once shared with the child's mother. As a result of her frustration, she used some harsh language and tones toward Joe. Sue expressed that Joe was a no-good man just like his father, and she was not sure why she gave him the time of day. Those words cut Joe deep and wide. No matter what happened moving forward, the relationship would never be the same. A man's number one basic need is respect, and when men are not honored, they shut down, retaliate, and sometimes get involved in extramarital affairs. Whenever we speak from emotions rather than a rational perspective, we can cause irreparable damage. That conversation just might have been their last.

COULD JOE HAVE DONE SOMETHING DIFFERENT?

Women's number one need is security, and when we men speak, we must keep this in mind if we desire to connect with them. Under these circumstances, whatever Joe could have done might not have been sufficient. Let's revisit this situation with another approach.

In the first example, Joe received his phone call and said he had to go see about his child, and he headed out the door. What if he'd handled the minutes after he received the call with a little more consideration for Sue's basic needs? What if he'd said his child's mother was taking his child to the emergency room. The child had a temperature of 104, and she was not sure what was wrong. He was heading to the emergency room, and she was more than welcome to come. If she didn't want to, he would call with an update as soon as he got there and got word of the child's condition.

In this case, Joe would have shown far more sensitivity toward Sue's basic need for security. Based on words like these, Sue would have had no reason to believe Joe had any other motive to leave than the health and welfare of his child. Just maybe if this approach was taken, it could have prevented their damaging exchange of words.

Let me note, if a relationship is missing trust, there may not be an approach that will ever be good enough. The goal is always to seek higher ground and to sleep with a good conscience, knowing you did the right thing. We can't control someone else actions; we can only control how we respond. Every situation calls for an equal or opposite reaction. No matter what circumstances we find ourselves in, we always have to be conscious of how we respond. When we are faced with adverse situations in our relationships, they have a way of revealing our character. No matter how frustrated we get, we should always respond with respect, because once something is stated, we cannot take it back.

Rules of Engagement

To minimize the opportunity to be disrespectful during disagreements, my wife and I came up with a few rules of engagement. These rules also centralize our discussion and keep both parties on an even playing field.

- What's on the table stays on the table. This means nothing else is brought into the conversation until what's on the table has been resolved. In other words, one issue at a time.
- I agree not to use disparaging words toward you.
- I agree not to bring up a prior offense, especially when it's to avoid taking ownership of my issue.
- What's in the past stays in the past!
- If I have forgiven you, I can't hold that over your head to keep you in prison.

- I agree to attempt to make it easy for you to summarize my problem. I will not talk at length, which will cut down on the chance of adding other items unintentionally to the agenda.
- I will not use the words *never* or *always,* because they are absolutes.
- I will always remember that our relationship represents something far greater than us. We are God's representatives.

What are some of your rules of engagement?

Do you handle disagreements with respect for one another?

Is there an issue that's been discussed that you really haven't forgiven each other for?

Takeaways

- You're both worthy of respect.
- Treat each other the way you want to be treated.
- Be conscious of how you respond to things that trigger your emotional state.

CHAPTER 11

Never Go to Bed Mad

You shall know the truth, and the truth shall make you mad.

~ Aldous Huxley

In June of 2009, I was headed to Meridian, Mississippi, for my twenty-five-year class reunion. It was hard to believe it had been twenty-five years since I'd graduated high school. Excitement filled my body with the anticipation of visiting with old friends and talking about our high school days.

Every time I ran into my classmates, they would always remind me of our senior talent show when Tabitha Adams, Cathy Hellen, and I performed to the hit single "Thriller." I can still remember all the days we practiced, attempting to get the routine perfect. As we were standing behind the curtains before our performance, fear and anticipation filled our bodies. When we saw the number of people in the audience, our trepidation increased. The crowd cheered so loudly that we couldn't hear the music. We had practiced so intently that the routine was second nature with or without the music. There's nothing like having hundreds of people scream about your performance. That's a high which is hard to come down from, and a difficult moment to forget. I think we all felt like celebrities.

I was still thinking about that day when I was close to the Louisiana border, when the radio stopped playing to give some breaking news. I was in the car dancing and listening to old school music, and the radio announcement broke my rhythm. I assumed that whatever the news was, it would not affect me. Boy, was I wrong. The DJ announced that singer, dancer, and songwriter Michael Jackson had just died. At first I thought someone was playing a cruel joke, until I noticed every radio station was covering this story. How could this be? He was only fifty, and he'd still had so much life to live and so much to offer the world. I was devastated. Yet again, the demise of someone who meant so much to me was a reminder of my mortality.

The Day That Changed My World

It was the summer of 2012. Darrell Malone, a hometown friend, called because he couldn't get in contact with my brother, Larry. He stated that each time he called, his phone went to voicemail. My brother was notorious for not answering his phone, but he would always return a call. This caused immediate concern.

I called my cousin Cathy, who lived about ten minutes from my brother, and asked could she go by and check on him. It was dark when I called Cathy, so she went by the next day. She noticed when she arrived that his car was not parked out front, so she assumed he was not home. She rang the doorbell, but no one answered. The door was unlocked, but it was latched. As she pushed the door open, she was greeted with an unbearable smell of decaying flesh.

The unthinkable just became our reality. At fifty-seven years of age, my brother's existence had come to an abrupt end. My brother was ten years my senior and was more like a father than a brother. He was my role model and mentor. As I am writing these words, tears are forming in my eyes because it's still hard to swallow. His death marked an indelible moment that would forever alter my life. Questions that haunted me were:

> When was the last time I spoke with him?
> Did I tell him that I loved him often enough?
> Did he know I loved him?
> When was the last time I saw him?
> Could I have done more?
> Was I involved with him enough?

We all realize that life offers no guarantees other than death and taxes. Every day we hear of someone's demise, and I'm sure most of the dead had no idea death would call their name that day. Growing up, I would always hear older people saying to give them flowers while they could appreciate them. Unfortunately, I had no idea what this meant and how it would resonate with me years later.

We hope for tomorrow, but in reality, we only have this very moment.

Several years ago, I conducted a marriage seminar at a local church. As I was concluding my talk, a gentleman entered the room. I was completing my segment on never going to bed mad; however, he hadn't heard what had preceded those comments. I overheard the gentleman telling someone that wasn't possible, that you just can't resolve everything before you go to bed.

Does he have a point?

Can we resolve our issues before our heads hit the pillow?

Why is not going to bed mad important?

STINKING THINKING

What we desire doesn't drive our behavior. What we believe does. If we don't believe or think something is possible, we will not put forth the necessary effort to make it a reality.

> *"Whether you think you can or can't, either way, you are right." ~ Henry Ford*

A negative and defeated attitude is a result of stinking thinking that can contaminate us and anything in proximity.

> *Our greatest impediment to success is our disbelief that we can.*

LIVING WHAT I PREACH

I will be the first to admit: to never go to bed mad is extremely challenging, as most goals worth obtaining are. From time to time my wife and I might not see eye to eye, and we go to bed mad, but that is never our intention. Our goal is to resolve all issues before our heads hit the pillow, but even our marriage is not free from fault. But because this is part of what we have vowed, going to bed mad is infrequent in our relationship. Without goals, like never going to bed mad, a better way will never become a reality.

WHY NOT GO TO BED MAD?

No matter how hard we try, we can't escape our consciences. Whether we go from one end of the earth to another, we can't outrun it. Having a condemned conscience can sometimes be worse than being in prison. Depending upon the crime, prisoners know when they will be released, but when our consciences are condemned, we have no idea when we will get some reprieve.

THE HARSH REALITY

What if my spouse did not wake up the following morning? Would the disagreement we had the night before still be relevant? At this point, would it matter who was right and who was wrong? Because she didn't do what I wanted, am I still holding her accountable? One of my biggest fears is going to bed mad and never being given another opportunity to reconcile. When someone passes, we don't get a do over. I can't speak for you, but I don't want to live with that situation on my conscience for the rest of my life. This is why our goal is always to reconcile before we go to bed—because most situations are just not that serious.

If we never make not going bed mad a priority, it's not possible for it to become our reality. All we have is this moment. The choice is ours as to what we are going to do with it.

How often do you go to bed without reconciling with each other?

Can you live with the idea of something happening to your spouse knowing you had the opportunity to reconcile but didn't?

What can you do to minimize the times you go to bed mad?

Takeaways

- Each day you spend with a loved one could be your last—spend the time wisely.

CHAPTER 12

Be a Constant Investor

Be not deceived; God is not mocked: for whatsoever a man soweth, that shall he also reap. ~ *Galatians 6:7*

Farming doesn't get a lot of attention, but it is one of the most needed occupations in our culture. Living in Texas, I pass by crops all the time and give little consideration to the time and effort that goes into producing a good harvest. Farmers work tirelessly year round so that when we go to get groceries, we can have fresh vegetables. I'm grateful I'm able to reap the benefits of what they've sown.

It Comes with a Price

If farmers are to reap from what they have sown, they must first plant. It would be ludicrous if a farmer went outside to harvest a crop he had not planted. However, after they have planted, farmers understand that planting is only the beginning. For the farmer to get the desired return on his investment, it's going to take more investing. The crop he just planted is going to take a little nurturing to produce an increase. Just as much as the farmer desires an increase, there are various impediments he has to also consider. In Texas, there are some summers when we go months without rain, or we experience inclement weather. And as you might already suspect, produce attracts insects and animals.

WHAT WE FEED GROWS AND WHAT WE STARVE DIES

If the farmer does everything perfectly, there is still no guarantee he will reap a great harvest. However, you can be sure that if he doesn't invest time and care in the crop, it will not produce a great harvest. Reaping and sowing are not just a biblical principle, but a principle we are living consciously or unconsciously every day. The success of our marriages depends upon our commitment to sowing—the marriage will reap from what's been planted.

What are you feeding your marriage?

How does sowing and reaping relate to your marriage?

Professional Occupations

Robert goes to the hospital for a simple outpatient procedure. As he is about to be treated, his doctor explains that he has not had any additional training since med school, which was twenty-two years ago. He claims he doesn't need any more because he's smart. Naturally, Robert asks for a different doctor.

Of course, this is a fictitious story, because doctors are required to take continuing courses every year to keep learning and investing in their skills. The human body is complex, and with all of our medical advances, no one has mastered the body. As much as we have come to know about the body, there is so much we still do not know. Just think: there is still no cure for the common cold.

With the body being so multifaceted, I think the concerns Robert shared resonate with most of us. Occupational growth and advancement are crucial, and a requirement for most organizations. Companies understand that to remain relevant, they must invest in the development of their greatest asset—their people.

BOB THE MECHANIC

What if Bob the mechanic, who died in the seventies, were alive today? He would be at a loss working on today's computer-driven cars. Cars are far more complicated, and mechanics who have refused to keep up with all the advances have found themselves out of work or scarcely employed. I was speaking to Dewayne of Genuine Car Care in Leander, Texas, and he told me he will not hire mechanics who won't agree to invest in their personal and professional development. He understands that anyone refusing to grow will not be beneficial to the growth of his business.

Something to Ponder

Several months ago, I met with a local pastor to discuss conducting some leadership and marriage workshops with his church. This pastor was highly educated and worked at one of the most prestigious universities in the country. After a few minutes of dialogue, I asked him, "With all the education you have obtained, how many courses have you taken regarding relationships and leadership?" He responded, "None." Leadership and marriage courses are not taught at length at most schools. If we are not intentional about learning and growing, we will have a difficult time trying to lead within our relationships.

What about Your Marriage?

Unfortunately, there is no requirement for us to invest in our marriages. No one is knocking on our doors asking us about the last time we attended a marriage workshop, read a book on marriage, or went to counseling. If we don't make investing in our marriage a nonnegotiable, it will not happen. Unwillingness to invest in growth, as well as marriage, will cause couples to slowly grow apart. Some won't know when it happened, but one day they will look at their partners with the strangest look because they'll realize they are living with complete strangers. Most of us have probably heard couples say they have just grown apart. If we don't choose to grow together, we're choosing to grow apart.

Some couples attend counseling before marriage to obtain an outside perspective. They understand that some underlying issues need to be uncovered before they say *I do.* Most religious institutions require members to attend premarital counseling before the pastor agrees to conduct the ceremony. Unfortunately, this is the last investment most couples will make in their marriage. Couples that attend counseling after the ceremony are usually in a crisis and very seldom visit for preventive measures. After years of verbal abuse, infidelity, parental issues, and troubled finances, their circumstances dictate a need for intervention. When things get this far out of control, it is complicated to put things back on the right path.

Your Marriage Is Worth Your Investment

Success does not occur by happenstance; it has to be fed intentionally. People who have prodigious marriages have suffered, endured, and invested in their marriages to have a relationship worthy of recognition. Whether you have been married for years or you're newlyweds, I strongly suggest making investing in your marriage a priority. The only way relationships become significant and remain great is by making an intentional decision to have ongoing investments to make them great. So where do we start?

START WITH A BOARD OF DIRECTORS

Most companies have a board of directors, a group of individuals elected to act as representatives of the stockholders. They establish corporate management related policies and make decisions on major company issues.

If companies can have a board that represents the best interests of the stockholders, why can't you have a board of directors that represents the best interests of your marriage? The good thing about having a board of directors for your marriage is that people don't have to know they are on your board. However, I don't encourage picking just anyone to be on your board. Choose people who will add value to your marriage and hold you accountable.

How does this work? Find a couple with a marriage you would like to mimic and take them out to dinner, or just sit and converse. Watch how they interact with each other and ask questions. Most people take great pride talking about their success. When people don't know they are on your board, you get authentic and transparent responses. Ask your new board members to meet on a weekly, biweekly, or monthly basis. Most couples will be delighted and honored that you want to meet with them. It's important to let them know you appreciate their time and, as you make progress, share your success with them. Please be aware that most people don't want to share their time and insights with people who do not intend to change. Make sure you are ready to do, and be, something different.

Board of Directors for Your Kids

No matter how many books we read about parenting, it is not a simple task. The good news is that we don't have to parent alone. Most of us know people who have children we would like our children to grow up to be like and reflect. Hopefully, you have already anticipated my next statement. You guessed it: Make them part of your board of directors.

Whenever we want to improve any aspect of our marriage or life, we find a couple who is where we want to be and place them on our board of directors. Contrary to popular belief, we were never intended to go it alone. Let someone who is where you desire to be freely invest in your marriage. This is how we go further faster. I know what some of you might be thinking at this point: *This means I'm going to have to open up to another couple.* Yes, but only after your spouse and you feel comfortable and know that your newly appointed board members have your best interests at heart. The good news is you will not be sharing anything new, because they have already crossed the road you are trying to cross. To get to where you want to be, you have to be willing to do something you have never done.

> DID YOU NOTICE? On the front cover of this book is a couple holding hands, and under those hands is someone else holding both of their hands together. This is the person who will support, counsel, and walk with them on their journey. When we ask someone to hold us accountable and offer his or her support, it is a good indication that we are serious about succeeding in marriage.

WAKE-UP CALL

While you are finding couples that will invest in your marriage, please be reminded that there is nothing wrong with your marriage. What? Yes, there is nothing wrong with your marriage. The goal is to work on the *people* in the marriage, and the marriage will fix itself.

The Ultimate Test of Your Growth

During an interview, the hiring manager asked me if I had any questions, so I asked him how I would be better that time next year because he was leading me. He gave me the deer in the headlights look. I believe the ultimate test of leaders is not how great they have become, but how great they can make those around them. Michael Jorden is considered by many to be the greatest basketball player ever to play the game. Some of his accomplishments include:

- Member of six NBA championship teams (1991–93, 1996–98)
- Five-time NBA Most Valuable Player (1988, 1991–92, 1996, 1998)
- Six-time NBA Finals Most Valuable Player (1991–93, 1996–98)
- Ten-time All-NBA First Team (1987–93, 1996–98)
- All-NBA Second team (1985)
- Nine-time NBA All-Defensive First Team (1987–93, 1996–98)
- NBA Defensive Player of the Year (1988)
- NBA Rookie of the Year (1985)
- NBA All-Rookie Team (1985)
- Two-time IBM Award winner, for all-around contribution to team's success (1985, 1989)
- Three-time NBA All-Star Game MVP (1988, 1996, 1998)

~ National Basketball Association[1]

Even if you are not a basketball fan, you must admit these are some extraordinary accomplishments. However, in my humble opinion, these achievements are not what made him the greatest to ever play the game. What made him great was his ability to make everyone around him greater. This is a great leadership tip for all you great leaders. It is not about how great we become, but how great we make others. So what does this have to do with marriage?

Make Another Couple Better

Once someone has invested in you and your marriage, return the favor and invest in someone else. If you can duplicate with someone else the growth you have experienced, we can change the world one marriage at a time. Most people wait until their marriage is hitting on all eight cylinders before they will even consider mentoring another couple. However, the best time to invest in someone else is when you are not at your best. This will make you accountable to the couple you have chosen to mentor. And because none of us want to be hypocrites, you will work diligently to ensure you are living what you are teaching.

What couple can you invest in?

Will you use counseling as a preventive measure and not just on an as-needed basis?

What couple will you choose to be on your board of directors?

Why is investing in your marriage so important?

DON'T WAIT UNTIL YOU FEEL LIKE IT; DO IT AND YOU'LL FEEL LIKE IT

Whether you've been married for a while or you are recently married, I hope to inspire you to take a different approach to a successful marriage. Marriages are under attack, and most couples are succumbing to the pressures of these attacks. Divorce lawyers have become more popular than marriage counselors. Every day I see billboards advertising lawyers who are waiting for you to file for divorce. Our children are being raised in single-parent households and being exposed to multiple relationships. As a result, they are growing up with various emotional issues that could be avoided. Our finances are being ruined, and many couples have to file for bankruptcy. Investing allows us to grow together, whereas not investing makes it possible to grow apart.

What if today you and I agreed that our marriages were worth the investment? I want divorce lawyers to have fewer clients so they have to practice a different type of law. This is not an easy journey, because you are surrounded by people who don't take their vows seriously. However, you are a leader, and someone has to be willing to set a new standard. Why not make yourself that person? You might not feel like investing, but once you start, you'll feel like it. I'm confident that together we will make a difference, starting with our marriages and then with our intentional investments in other people's marriages. We invest in our cars, homes, and occupations. I think it's time for us all to put that type of effort into our marriages. We'll appreciate the return, and it's worth the effort.

Takeaways

Your mission is what you are doing.
Your vision is where you are going.
Your core values are your guiding principles.
Divorce is not an option.
We are one financial institution, we vow sexual exclusion etc., are all our systems and processes. They aid in making our mission, vision, and core values our reality.

It is easy to get married, but the challenge is staying married, which takes intentionality. Success in marriage will never happen by happenstance but rather by two people who are purposely driving themselves to succeed. Marriage is under attack in our society, and we have to be equipped with the tools to fight back.

For my wife and me, one of the things that has made the greatest difference in our marriage is that we have agreed not to give up on each other, so the marriage has no choice but to succeed. Notice I didn't say give up on marriage. The goal in marriage or relationships is always to be working on self, and the marriage or relationship will benefit from your efforts.

When couples decide together that divorce is not an option, it minimizes turmoil. The hardest part about deciding is deciding. Once getting a divorce is not an option, it changes your approach toward marriage. Both feet are in the door at all times, and never is there a dilemma regarding staying or going. It's never a matter of *can we* work this out but *how* and *when.*

If you have not seriously invested in your marriage, my prayer is that this can be a start. Our children, coworkers, church family, neighbors, and community are looking for examples of healthy families. Often when we consider change, it's about changing what's outside us, but let's start by working on ourselves from the inside out. Let's be that example the world is longing to see.

> *Happiness in marriage is like a butterfly—the more you chase it, the more it eludes you; however, once you find your purpose and become intentional about succeeding in your marriage, happiness comes and sits softly on your shoulder.*

Notes

1 ~ http://www.nba.com/jordan/list_honors.html

About the Author

The youngest of five siblings, Richard grew up and graduated from high school in the small town of Meridian, Mississippi. Richard dropped out of college after two years and decided to join the United States Army. There, he began to gain valuable insights regarding leadership, relationships, teamwork, and commitment to something greater than self.

After serving proudly for twenty-three years, Richard reentered the marketplace. He was taken aback at the lack of leadership, people-building skills, and camaraderie he had enjoyed in the military. In response, Richard created Pathways, a leadership and relationship coaching organization, which is committed to helping people grow so they can intentionally assist in growing others. Richard is also an author and certified speaker, trainer, and coach with the John Maxwell Team.

Pathways Mission

To transform organizations by enhancing their existing culture through leadership systems and principles, thus creating change, growth, and profitability. We believe when you enhance your culture, you change your results.

Welcome to Pathways, where change is closer than you think.

Other books by Richard

Leadership in Life and Love

Contact Richard

Pathways with Richard E. Hellen offers:

- Leadership Development
- Team Building
- Business Development
- Relationship Coaching
- Business Coaching
- Keynote Speaking Services
- CDs and video materials on leadership available

Contact Richard Hellen to learn more:
Web: www.rhpathways.com
Tel: 512-786-8823
E-mail: info@Pathways.com

Acknowledgements

I'd like to thank my wife, Kim Hellen, for showing me that unconditional love is possible. At one point in my life, I had given up on love, but God introduced you to me, proving he is still in the prayer-answering business. You could have easily been turned off by my past, but God allowed you to see my heart. My only regret is that we did not meet sooner, so I could have had additional time to love you. It probably goes without saying that no journey comes without challenges, but you realized those challenges existed to make our relationship stronger. My prayer is that God will enable us to continue to love each other with his unconditional love and be an example to our children and the world. I'm looking forward to many more years of loving, laughing, and making you smile, because the best is yet to come.

I want to thank my children, Kanesha Johnson, Lashunda (Nunu) Johnson, and Jahari Hellen for supporting and giving our marriage your blessing. We are honored and never want to take your support for granted. Our prayer is to continue to be positive examples so that you have no excuse for not succeeding relationally. We understand that one day you will introduce us to ourselves in the people that you are going to become when you date or marry. Hopefully we have demonstrated what we have always preached.

I want to thank Leonard and Yolanda Rhem for always being an example to follow. Your love for each other and your commitment to your marriage has always been unwavering. My prayer is that God will continue to use you as an example, because the ministry is in dire need for what you have to share. Looking forward to the day (if it's his will) that you call me and tell me you started your ministry.

I would like to thank Harry and Lendy Jones for your faithful commitment to each other. It's a blessing to see couples with your tenure and know you still like each other. I look at you as an example that longevity and contentment are possible.

And last but not least, Mommy and Poppy Santos. I never will forget the day I saw you, Mommy, looking sad because Poppy had to travel alone to see his family and you were unable to be with him, and you were miserable. You have been married for more than thirty years, and you are just as in love today as you were the day you married. Your marriage has proved that longevity is possible, and your love for each other is apparent. It's rare in our culture to see someone who's been married for more than thirty years and is still madly in love. Our prayer is to replicate your example. Thanks for being a positive example.

It's because of all of you that I have the confidence that success in marriage is possible.

Richard & Kim Hellen

TEAM HELLEN

Recommended Reading

Seven books on marriage

The Bible

Gray, John. *Men Are from Mars, Women Are from Venus.* New York City: HarperCollins.

Chapman, Gary. *The Five Love Languages.* Chicago: Northfield Publishing.

Eggerichs, Dr. Emerson. *Love and Respect Workbook.* Nashville: Thomas Nelson.

Kendrick, Stephen and Alan. *The Love Dare.* Nashville: B&H Books.

Maxwell, John C. *Everyone Communicates but Few Connect.* Nashville: Thomas Nelson.

Silk, Danny. *Keep Your Love On.* Redding: Loving on Purpose.

79976537R00105

Made in the USA
Lexington, KY
28 January 2018